2ND EDITION

Practice Management Guide

Published by RICS Business Services Limited
a wholly owned subsidiary of
The Royal Institution of Chartered Surveyors
under the RICS Books imprint
Surveyor Court
Westwood Business Park
Coventry CV4 8JE
UK

No responsibility for loss occasioned to any person acting or refraining from action as a result of the material included in this publication can be accepted by the author or publisher.

First published in 1997

ISBN 1 84219 136 5

HSE material reproduced by kind permission of the HSE

Typeset in Great Britain by Columns Design Limited, Reading
Printed in Great Britain by Q3 Litho, Loughborough

Contents

RICS Guidance Notes

This is a guidance note. It provides advice to members of RICS on aspects of the profession. Where procedures are recommended for specific professional tasks, these are intended to embody 'best practice', that is, procedures which in the opinion of RICS meet a high standard of professional competence.

Members are not required to follow the advice and recommendations contained in the guidance note. They should, however, note the following points.

When an allegation of professional negligence is made against a surveyor, the court is likely to take account of the contents of any relevant guidance notes published by RICS in deciding whether or not the surveyor has acted with reasonable competence.

In the opinion of RICS, a member conforming to the practices recommended in this guidance note should have at least a partial defence to an allegation of negligence by virtue of having followed those practices. However, members have the responsibility of deciding when it is appropriate to follow the guidance. If it is followed in an inappropriate case, the member will not be exonerated merely because the recommendations were found in an RICS guidance note.

On the other hand, it does not follow that a member will be adjudged negligent if he or she has not followed the practices recommended in this guidance note. It is for each individual chartered surveyor to decide on the appropriate procedure to follow in any professional task. However, where members depart from the good practice recommended in this guidance note, they should do so only for good reason. In the event of litigation, the court may require them to explain why they decided not to adopt the recommended practice.

In addition, guidance notes are relevant to professional competence in that each surveyor should be up to date and should have informed him or herself of guidance notes within a reasonable time of their promulgation.

Introduction

Yes, but what are we actually going to do?

That question, asked by a partner of a successful practice, summed up the mood of the first meeting of the project that was to become these 'guidelines'. Eleven partners had volunteered to participate in an innovative experiment organised by the Royal Institution of Chartered Surveyors (RICS) with backing from the government's 'Skills Challenge' programme. We aimed, over the next year, to distil their collective experience into a series of guidelines for use by the profession as a whole; guidelines which would cover business and managerial rather than professional issues.

The discussion which followed established several criteria which the project was to follow:

- **Keep it short and simple**. We would aim at plain English.

- Recognise **each practice is very different.**

- **Do not dictate**. We were not seeking a set of mandatory guidelines or an 'instant recipe' for success. Instead we would seek to define key questions that partners could ask themselves about their own practice.

- **Base it on real life**.

We then discussed how best to subdivide the complex business of managing a modern practice into a list. What do partners do as leaders and managers? In the end it seemed quite simple, at least in theory. They ensure that the 'people' in the practice operate with systems and procedures that deliver – to chosen clients – what those clients want, hence our Practice Management Model (shown below).

How then to break the guidelines down?

We decided on six main topics:

- Developing a **Practice Strategy**.

- Reviewing and monitoring **Client Service and Marketing**.

- **Leadership** and an understanding of people, as individuals and as a 'culture' in the practice.

- **Benchmarking and Learning**: positioning the practice to be successful in the future.

- Internal **Policies and Procedures**.

- **Practice finance** and financial planning.

Each become the subject of a further workshop. Each workshop had a similar format. We, as project co-ordinators (and subsequently the authors of this document), arranged a draft set of guidelines or questions based on – but simplified from – existing standards, especially those embodied in the National Vocational standards for owner management, the ISO 9000 Quality Assurance framework and the Investors In People (IIP) scheme. We also produced a background paper synthesising relevant theory and practice and invited two case studies from consortium members.

Armed with the case studies, and presentations on the background theory, the group of eleven and guests (see *Appendix 3*) then reviewed the draft guidelines and suggested changes and improvements. It proved to be a formula that worked. Through the case studies, the members discovered that they all had things to learn from each other about managing their own practices. The RICS gained a set of guidelines that were tested with real life partners in successful small to medium practices.

Finally, we went over the guidelines one last time to produce a synthesis of the key issues; a summary (presented here as *Guideline 7*) for people who are considering setting up in practice on their own account, or who have recently done so.

Throughout the document we refer to 'partners' and 'the practice' as the key audiences for the lessons of experience. We do, however, believe the concepts are also highly applicable to chartered surveyors working 'in-house' or with public sector organisations.

Yes, but how can I use these guidelines?

All the hard thinking, all the questions, serve no purpose unless people in the practice are prepared to do things differently as a result. It is a natural tendency to spend more time on the parts of a job that we enjoy. Making any change will require effort in areas that we are prone to avoid. So how will you make it happen?

Two possible ways of initiating such change using these *Guidelines* could involve:

- partners, or indeed anyone in the practice considering the future of the practice, to conduct, using these questions, their own appraisal of the firm/department's competitive position,

- for a firm, in the strict or general sense of the word, to prepare, using these *Guidelines*, for a strategic review of the pratice's competitive position and future strategy.

If more than one person is involved we suggest that each 'stakeholder' considers the questions and uses the insights gained as the foundation of shared discussions. Successful practice development, especially changes of strategy, takes joint work.

The objective is to encourage partners and others to think about their perceptions about the practice. The next task is to consider, collectively, the insight(s) gained and determine what, if any, changes are desirable.

The steps are, in essence, to decide:

Where the practice is now,

Where you intend it to be,

What needs doing.

We believe that it is important in your professional life to give these questions the same attention as you give to client business. Not a brief planning meeting at 5pm or a quick chat over a few sandwiches at lunch-time (although both will help), but some core time when everyone can contribute by giving this their full attention for a reasonable period of time. One possible approach which involves a one-day retreat is outlined in *Appendix 2*.

Further details about the authors can be found in *Appendix 3*.

Tom Kennie
Ranmore Consulting Group
If Price
Sheffield Hallam University
Project co-ordinators and authors of the *Guidelines*

Practice
Management
Guideline 1

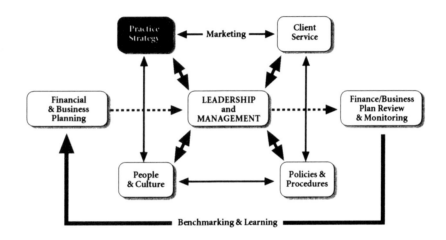

Practice Strategy
and Structure

*Have you developed
an explicit strategy
for your practice?*

Background Principles: Guideline 1 Practice Strategy and Structure

A recent search for 'strategy' at Amazon.com yielded 8067 titles using that word. Yet there are no clear-cut answers as to what strategy is, or more importantly how one is set for a particular practice. This short summary provides a primer to the major schools of opinion on strategy and some suggestions as to lessons for the professional practice. In fact, most books and articles on the topic ignore the practice and aim firmly at the market for large, multi-divisional corporations.

The classical rational school of strategic planners, with Michael Porter as their best known exponent, argued that strategic choice could be made following rational analysis of markets in terms of the five forces of supplier power, customer power, competitors, technological threats, and entry barriers. Strategy was almost a matter of economic market analysis. Firms could position products and even divisions as future stars (to be nurtured with investment), cash-cows (to be milked) or dogs (to be discarded). Especially over the last 20 years, but with earlier antecedents, that view has been challenged.

Observers of actual management behaviour in decision making, notably Henry Mintzberg, saw managerial rationality bounded by circumstance and prevailing orthodoxy in a particular firm or industry. Strategy for them had a considerable herd effect and was in practice a pattern which emerged from a stream of decisions. In Mintzberg's words, 'the only people to have benefited from strategic planning are the strategic planners'. Other researchers went further and included wider social patterns appertaining to a particular country as influencing the stream of decisions actually made. Among those achieving 'guru' status from following these lines of argument were Peter Senge, asserting the need for firms to cultivate practices or 'disciplines' which helped them surface and challenge prevailing 'mental models'; and Richard Pascale who asserted, in 1990, that the work of managers should be 'making and breaking paradigms'. 'Instead', he went on, 'we devote 99% of our efforts to squeezing more and more out of the existing paradigm and it's killing us'.

During the 1990s, a new wave of strategic commentators tried to resurrect what might be called a 'neo-rationale' school. Gary Hamel (then of London Business School) and CK Pralahad achieved considerable fame for their notion of 'core competencies': technologies or other special skills and knowledge which companies could leverage in many different products. Honda's skills in high speed engine technologies or Nike's brand management were frequently cited as examples. John Kay (then of Oxford Business School) argued for more generic sources of sustainable competitive advantage in terms of firm's market barriers, capacity for innovation and what he termed their 'architecture': the network of relationships within the firm and between the firm and its suppliers, collaborators and competitors. Indeed as the decade wore on, their was more talk of 'co-option', a term coined to try and highlight the fact that whether another firm was a competitor or a potential ally might depend on the circumstance of a particular market sector or opportunity.

Despite these advances, the understanding of the true nature of strategy remains elusive. Some of the examples used by Kay in 1995 as firms who had delivered outstanding economic value added in their sectors were, five years later, seen as 'troubled' or 'beleaguered', victims perhaps of their prior success or overconfidence. In fairness, the point does not disprove Kay's argument, it merely points out the difficulty of sustaining a capability to innovate where organisations possess a seemingly inherent tendency to preserve patterns of thinking that have lost their relevance to a particular market.

Does all this have any relevance for the smaller professional practice? In short, yes. In the course of the original *Practice Management Guidelines* project we had lengthy interviews with either the founder, the managing partner, or a senior partner about the practice's history and current market. Subsequently, we conducted a second series of *Practice Management Guidelines* workshops with another group of small, surveying, architectural and design professionals and we have used them to help a variety of businesses with their own development. Similar messages occur time and time again and we believe we can see a generic model of critical stages in the development of a practice. Not all, of course, make it through all of these.

Stage 1: the early years

Firms are founded when typically one or two individuals with particular professional knowledge, and more importantly, a particular set of contacts with key clients or suppliers decide to 'go-it-alone'. The strategy, if there is one, is often no more than the ad hoc exploitation of that niche while it lasts. Management is either the loose activity of a few key individuals, or the ad hoc influence of a dominant founder acting as a 'benevolent' dictator.

Firms at this stage may grow reasonably large, sometimes achieving professional employees numbered in tens, before the senior partner's span of control is exhausted and he or she has to delegate more responsibility for particular business segments or activities to another more junior partner. Frequently that partner may want to develop a strand of business away from the founder's 'core'.

Crisis 1: outliving the founder

One of our case study practices was still conducting most of its, obviously diminished, turnover in a market segment first entered by the founder in 1949. In another, the founder had seen his business rise to a 12-person practice then shrink again, unable to survive a recession. Several were still thriving under their first founder or founding partner. The others all spoke of the time in which they had made the transition, often with some pain, to a second stage of development when the founders had died, retired or moved on to new pastures.

Few firms seem to survive, and we have not met one that has prospered, by clinging to the original founder's specialities, even if more generic attributes and policies or attitudes do make it through. The need to generate new patterns of thought to move forward is evident.

Stage 2: new structures

With the founder departed, the growing practice faces the need to evolve a different managerial structure, when several partners, or other key individuals, are likely to be important. Numerous different models appear:

Revolving democracies – rotates any managerial co-ordination role between partners. It can be highly effective, but carries the risks that either, a practice develops a series of mini businesses which fail to develop and exploit any synergy, or that at a critical juncture, the partner in the chair exerts insufficient or inappropriate influence.

Management by representation – abandons any attempt at formal co-ordination substituting some loosely co-ordinated forum of heads of department. Provided the heads have a good working relationship with each other, see value in maintaining a common brand, and are subject to no serious threats to the status quo, this can be a very pleasant age to live in – unless you have under-performing departments, a deadbeat as a head or the number of departments grows significantly. Schisms can tear a firm apart as tensions rise between units with different apparent profitability. Responses to market shifts may be slow if it takes time for departmental heads to achieve a sufficient view of the threat and the need for change,

Crisis 2: developing a professional managerial culture

In firms which reach this stage, several key individuals have equity and/or significant intellectual property invested in the practice. In the future, some may want to realise that equity. As in any business managed for those who invest in it, a professional managerial structure is required. Not all the investors can participate in every decision. Again several solutions are tried.

Management by committee (and sub-committees) – tries to bring formality and discipline to a representational management structure with agendas and minutes and executive meetings held more frequently than full partnership meetings. Handled well, a committee structure can create the right balance between involvement and more rapid decision making. Allowed to take on a life of its own, it can lead to a sprawling myriad of small groups investigating all manner of issues – cars, salaries, marketing, training, pot-plant design in reception, the colour of the logo on the new brochure. This can then lead to:

Management by managing partner and management committee – as the need for improved co-ordination leads the partners to recognise that the committee needs to be chaired and actions need to be monitored. It is also apparent that some issues overlap and need to be more integrated. In some cases, conscious of their early experiences of the 'malevolent' dictator, reservations often exist about imbuing anyone with more 'power' and influence. Nevertheless, on balance the need arises and is often filled by someone who has already identified themselves as being both a respected professional and fee earner, and a good manager. The managing partner emerges. Again this age can be very successful – until the managing partner becomes frustrated and disillusioned. He/she can suddenly recognise they are now virtually full time on management and are no longer able to sustain their professional work.

They may also become increasingly frustrated at the type of activity they find themselves having to do – they need help, or else they evolve into:

Management by a management team – as the managing partner recognises the need for some professional support with the administration of the firm – a practice manager/partnership secretary. The added overhead is resisted by some, but, without this level of support, the firm is unlikely to progress and develop.

Over time the firm may grow further and an increasingly corporate structure emerges. The latter stages reflect the move towards an increasingly corporate structure.

Management by a chief executive, finance director and management board (not committee) – the introduction of the term chief executive, rather than managing partner, emphasises the nature of the power balance which exists within the firm at this stage. The CEO, if he/she is to be effective, now has an enhanced level of executive authority over the other partners, both implicitly and explicitly. Often partnership deeds are re-written at this stage to emphasise this change of relationship. The introduction of an individual into the firm from outside of the partnership may also occur at this stage. This adds to the power dynamic since, generally, the new CEO will not have a direct equity stake in the firm. To date, this model has proved to be a difficult one to sustain in the long term. However, in times of rapid change or crisis, this may prove to be a very effective structural change.

This level is also characterised by increasing levels of transparency and accountability. Formal business plans, performance review systems and so on will have become well established. Whilst collegial decision making will continue for some issues (and are essential for major issues, for example, a merger or major acquisition), the majority of decisions are made by a small number of senior managers.

By now, a further tension will be emerging as 'professionals as managers' become more aware of 'professional managers'. Professional managers, probably directors, will now have been appointed to take responsibility for a number of matters such as marketing and business development, human resources, IT, strategic planning, etc. Unless an effective means of reconciling the contribution of both groups can be achieved much wasted effort can occur as 'professional managers' attempt to exert authority over professional fee earners.

Crisis 3: managing the contribution of both professionals and professional managers

Firms which reach this stage, where managers are just that and are no longer necessarily fee earners are typically large with dominant brands and market positions. They are:

Public limited partnerships – plcs by name but a partnership by culture or true full-blown, listed public limited companies. The size of the organisation will have led to the establishment of separate operating companies in some 'group' formation. In addition, for many practices, the firm will now be international in scope, possibly with global aspirations. Structurally, the firm overall can no longer be managed in a collegial fashion – albeit the 'partner' concept may be retained. An executive board will make major strategic decisions with functional directors responsible for the strategic and operational management of their areas of expertise. Matters such as 'branding' and 'global integration' become of increasing significance. Which of the two forms proves most successful is a matter of current debate and, indeed, competition.

Each stage and style has its merits – but at certain points in the development of a firm it may find itself facing a new 'moment of truth' – when reorganisation to meet the firm's strategy becomes essential. The challenge is to recognise when the need is real and how to avoid it when it is illusory. The danger is continuing to cling to what has worked previously without questioning prior patterns and recipes.

The guidelines are designed to help you achieve that questioning process. Not all will be relevant at every stage, but at some point the shadow of the future looms.

Guideline 1: Have you developed an explicit strategy for your practice?

In a business environment in which the rate of change shows no sign of diminishing, the successful practice is likely to need to review periodically its strategic direction in order to set a context for more detailed business planning.

A professional practice has within it a portfolio of the skills, knowledge and capabilities of its members; a mix that includes not only special professional skills, and formal procedures, but also intangible assets such as the practice's presence and relationships in key business sectors, its reputation with clients or suppliers, and its 'culture' or 'way things are done'. The match or otherwise of that mix of capabilities to the market and the wider environment in which the practice operates determines its success or failure. A practice's strategy, either explicitly or implicitly, is the deployment of that capability mix in the wider environment in which the practice operates. It is often a product of past successes and even the traditions established by the founder or founding partners.

Strategic thinking, therefore, is the art and practice of examining the current fit of capabilities to the environment. Partners need to ensure that adequate, shared, intentions exist to keep the fit in the future. It may mean deploying existing capabilities differently and/or developing new ones.

The questions start by asking how well the partners understand that each other's aspirations for their relationship is crucial. They go on to encourage identification of what it is that makes the firm successful now and in the future and what might be preventing it from identifying new opportunities.

1.1 Are the aspirations, abilities and relationships of the existing owner(s) clearly understood?

- Has each partner identified their personal aspirations and how they affect the practice's business?

- Does each partner appreciate the contribution of their personal skills and capabilities to the practice's current business?

- Do the partners appreciate the contribution each makes to the success of the business?

Practices may choose to define 'partner' for these purposes in either the strict business sense or as a broader term embracing all the people key to the implementation of the strategy.

1.2 Is the current match of the practice's capabilities to its market understood?

- Is there a clear, shared, understanding of how the practice's existing capabilities serve its existing market: for example, through a well developed business plan that identifies what gives the practice its distinctive edge?

- Do the partners appreciate the dependence of that plan on their, and others', skills and knowledge?

- What do the partners see as the critical success factors to delivering the current business plan? Do they appreciate what provides their current competitive advantage?

- What is the current financial situation of the practice and its likely earnings and investment requirements in the next three years?

- How might the practice's market position be eroded in the future by new competitors or new demands from the market?

- What do you plan to do about any such erosion of your edge in the market?

1.3 Are the external trends that might affect the practice's future business identified and understood?

- Has the practice considered, or researched, the likely changes in the main markets for its products and services?

- Does the practice have plans to improve its services, target new markets, or change its share of existing markets? Does it have confirmation that the anticipated demand for its services will exist?

- Are the practice's plans translated into goals and targets (financial or otherwise) which it aims to achieve in the next three years (or other appropriate strategic time frame)? How does it plan to review those in the light of changing business climates?

- What are the strengths and weaknesses of your main competitors?

- What are the strengths, weaknesses and aspirations of your collaborators?

- What are the strengths and weaknesses of your main clients?

- What are your own relative strengths and weaknesses?

1.4 Does the practice understand which unwritten traditions, of its own, its market, or its professional speciality, help it to operate and which restrict its success?

- What percentage of the practice's current income is derived from its original business sectors and services?

- Has the practice made an assessment of the possible changes in demand for those services over the next strategic period?

- Has the practice assessed whether there is a changing demand for its services and whether there is a presumption that clients will continue to value the same expertise as they have previously done?

- Has the practice evaluated the need to acquire new skills and knowledge?

Practical Application Case Study: Strategy and Structure

Client A is a medium- to large-sized multidisciplinary firm. The firm operates in a well defined geographical region. Strategically, its reputation locally could be stated as 'quality service at modest fee rates'. In its regional market, the firm gained more than its fair share of high profile instructions. Regularly, however, it lost out (not on price) against two or three of the large national practices against which it had to compete for work involving the larger multinationals operating in the area.

Structurally, the firm was managed by a small management committee which was chaired by the managing partner. This reported to the full equity partnership which was chaired by the senior partner. Professional support was limited to a partnership secretary who also held the post of finance director, IT director and, when necessary, HR director.

The firm was also at a critical succession period – with the senior partner retiring in the very near future and the managing partner keen to delegate more responsibility to others on the management committee and identify a successor.

All three of these agendas were critical to the firm's long-term aspirations to grow its market share.

Using the *Practice Management Guidelines* as a diagnostic framework, a series of facilitated workshops were held with both the management committee and the broader partnership. A clear agenda of issues emerged and a process of more explicit business planning was introduced for all of the business units. In addition, a 'balanced scorecard' of performance criteria were identified. Over a period of six months, a much more clearly articulated set of plans were created.

In parallel, using the framework for evaluating where the practice was structurally, the management committee recognised the need for the firm to invest in additional professional management support, partly to support the managing partner and also to relieve the partnership secretary of an increasingly heavy workload. In addition, the process led to the identification of a managing partner (elect) to act as a deputy to the existing senior partner.

The *Guidelines* in this case provided a framework to help the management committee identify a range of elements which required integrating into a coherent strategy.

Practice
Management
Guideline 2

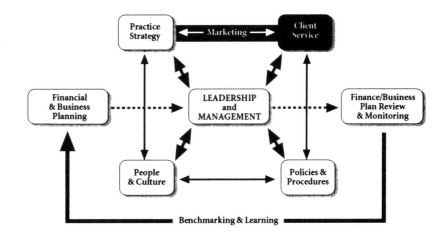

Marketing and
Client Service

Do your services and
service levels
match market needs?

Background Principles: Guideline 2 Marketing and Client Service

'Of all the business disciplines involved in running a modern legal practice, marketing remains the most difficult for partners to conquer. Confusion about what is meant by the word 'marketing' remains widespread.'

(*Marketing for Lawyers 2nd Edition*, Moore, Law Society Practice Handbooks, 1994)

'Selling focuses on the need of the seller. Marketing focuses on the needs of the buyer' (Levitt, 1975)

Marketing, anticipating the requirements of a particular segment of customers, and delivering products/services and associated 'images' to fit, is well established in the production of consumer goods and services. Textbooks, courses, and consultant advice abound. In professional services, there is, as the first quotation above illustrates, a widely held assumption that marketing is important but less clarity as to what it means or how the firm should go about it.

Our approach, focuses instead on marketing as the link between strategy – matching your capabilities to the needs of particular clients – your delivery of effective client service and the wider management of client relationships. In this sense, marketing concerns understanding, anticipating, and responding to the needs of clients and giving them a perception of what you can do for them. Our first diagram summarises this:

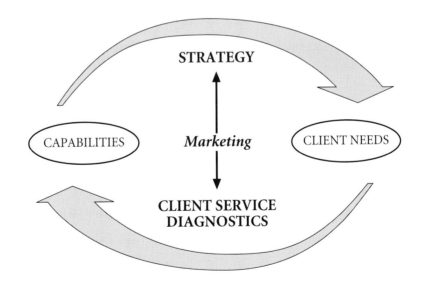

Figure 1

By comparing some other definitions:

- 'The management process of anticipating, identifying and satisfying customer requirements profitably' (*Chartered Institute of Marketing*) from which one might conclude marketing is the be all and end all of management

- 'The management of the relationship between the firm and its clients, existing and potential, to achieve the partner's practice objectives' (Moore 1994), and

- 'Building competitive and sustainable long term customer relationships which give continuing value to both parties',

it can be seen that they point to:

- knowing the clients you want to serve, and the services you offer (see Strategy), and
- maintaining existing relationships and developing new ones.

Most marketing text books cover a range of management activities from strategy – assessing capabilities and markets, through 'advertising' and 'promotion', 'selling' and 'tendering' to 'interpersonal relationships and 'service quality'. We have tried to keep this element simple:

Strategy	–	Deciding what message to get across
Marketing	–	Getting the message across
Client Service Feedback	–	Checking how well the message hit the target
Relationship Management	–	Ensuring continuity and growth in the relationship

David Maister (*Managing the Professional Service Firm*, The Free Press, 1993) uses the comparison of marriage and seduction to highlight the approach many professional service firms take to marketing. Seduction – chasing a new client – often appears more exciting than maintaining an existing relationship. But existing relationships also need effort. Two good questions to ask are:

1   What percentage of non-billable 'marketing time' does your practice allocate to existing clients rather than new clients?

2   How does this compare with the amount of business you expect from them over the next three years discounted by the risk that you will succeed in winning that business?

The calculations can be made more sophisticated by repeating them for individual major accounts, by discounting projected future business to arrive at an Expected Monetary Value in today's money and by using even more sophisticated risk/reward calculations, available today on standard spreadsheets, to arrive at the Net Present Value of current investment[1]. You can also separate time and resources spent on 'generic' or 'overhead' marketing from time and money spent chasing either the right to qualify or specific bids and proposals. However, even 'back of an envelope' comparisons will give you an assessment of the balance between reward and effort.

---

[1] The EMV of a future income stream is its value today, assuming a certain projected interest rate.

The NPV of a future prospect is the sum of income generated multiplied by the probability of it being received.

All too often, Maister suggests, the unwritten rule prevails that 'current client work should be billable'. In effect, existing, valuable, clients are charged for what is given away free to prospective clients. He suggests, instead, three generic strategies for directing marketing efforts at existing clients:

1   making the client disposed to use you again

2   increasing the firm's capabilities to serve the client, and

3   finding the next engagement.

Note that you might be doing this anyway with some of your bigger clients, without even thinking of it as marketing. Your marketing budget may already be larger than you think! Note also, that item involves the interpersonal. Knowing the client's business and industry is necessary – would you buy assistance from someone who seemed to be learning at your expense – **but it is not enough**. Knowing the client as a person, and knowing the unwritten rules he has to operate to in his own firm may be equally important. [Later modules in this series will cover 'interpersonal skills' and 'unwritten rules' as separate topics.] Some large professional services firms have profited for years from equivalents of the old adage 'nobody ever got fired for choosing IBM'. It is sad, but true, that in certain markets, the buying decision may be made on the basis that the person making it can absolve themselves of personal responsibility and risk if something goes wrong. Leaving such cynicism aside, most purchasers of a professional service are bound to feel exposed. By the very nature of the service, they are having to buy something from someone who knows more than they do about what is on offer. Of course they want to be reassured that the person selling knows what they are talking about, but they do not want to be made to feel ignorant, or forced to learn the supplier's language. Maister again,

> 'The single most important talent in selling professional services is the ability to understand the purchasing process (not the selling process) **from the clients' perspective. Qualification is rational: Selection is personal.**'

The key to getting business is to get the client talking about their business. And, while the purchaser may be the real target, and the focus of the partner's attention, they are not the only source of information, nor is it only from the partner that they receive an impression. Your junior staff, who may be spending much more time with the client and his organisation than you do, may be much better placed to see the client's perspective and influence his image of you than you are. How do you draw them into the firm's marketing effort? How can you better manage the multiple links into your client's organisation from all levels in yours?

Even if you are concentrating most of your efforts on the highest potential clients – those you already have – there is a need to look outside. Without new business you are exposed and constrained.

So what tactics should you use?

Maister's suggested order of merit in marketing tactics is:

The first team	The second string	Clutching at straws
Small scale seminars	Community/professional activities	Publicity
Speeches at industry meetings	Networking with potential referral sources	Brochures
Articles in client oriented press (posh for show: trade for dough)	Newsletters	Ballroom scale seminars
Proprietary research		Direct mail/cold calls Sponsorship/advertising/ video brochures

Some firms might wish to add exhibitions (provided they are those that the clients actually visit – not those where exhibitors circulate around each other's stands), client relationship management programmes and others.

Of course, which you use is partly a function of your overall objective. Figure 2 illustrates how you might map some of these different tactics depending on whether you are seeking to enhance the 'awareness' or 'relationship' aspects of your marketing plan.

Marketing and Business Development

'Awareness Marketing'	'General Passive Advertising'	'Personalised Active Advertising' 'Focused PR'	Integrated Marketing Plan
	'Focused Direct Mail' 'Untargeted PR'	'Major Sponsorship' 'Large Scale Exhibitions'	'Articles' 'Newsletters' 'Jointly published Research'
	'Unfocused Direct Mail'	'Large Scale Presentations'	'Focused Seminars' 'CRM' 'Targeted Hospitality'

'Relationship Marketing'

Figure 2

Since 1995 when we published the original guidelines, of course, the big difference has become the web. Dot-bomb jokes aside it is there and it reduces the search costs for any product dramatically while extending your reach. Even a small practice can go international.

The rules above still apply. Is your web page useful to someone in a hurry? Are you sure they want the elaborate video clip at the beginning which may play alright to a dedicated office workstation attached to a high bandwidth server but downloads painfully slowly when your client is sitting in an airport lounge with a lap top? If you have something different to offer, clients will come back to your page. Otherwise they won't bother.

The image of the firm, the style of your letters, the decor of the office, the reception areas and the way the telephone is answered have always been part of marketing. First impressions last and dissatisfied customers don't come back. The web adds to that list. When did you last use your own home page?

Usually someone manages the marketing effort on behalf of the practice. He or she may be seen as 'doing the marketing'. That is a fallacy. Everyone is part of marketing the firm. If marketing is delegated to a marketing manager he or she must be involved in formulating the firm's strategy. Without knowing not only what is written in the business plan but the thinking that shapes the strategy, the marketing manager cannot manage the firm's marketing.

Have a budget for it, covering a specific allocation of time for all partners and fee earners and other costs. Marketing and business development is a matter for all professionals – relying on a few 'rainmakers' is no longer a sustainable business model for a practice. The less of that budget devoted to 'raspberry jam – spread over necessary generic marketing', the more effective you are likely to be. Focus the message you want to put across on places where the clients you want are likely to get the message you want.

The cost of professional advisers is not only the cost of their time. It is the cost of yours and equally the cost of not having them is the cost of you trying to do an inferior job. If you are seeking someone to help you with PR/brochures or advertising find a firm that seems as focused on their clients as you are, then treat them the way they want to be treated by your clients. If they are any good, they know more about their business than you do – so don't waste time 'second guessing'.

Above all, the marketing effort is linked to the strategy, to the shared 'glue' which keeps the firm together, and to the speed at which you learn and improve, from the outside world and within the practice.

Guideline 2: How good is your client service and how well do you market the practice?

A successful professional practice has, by definition, found a way to match its particular capabilities to one or more sectors of the market (*Guideline 1*). It will also be reacting to that market, ensuring that the services provided are what the market is demanding, and responding to, or anticipating, signals from clients as to changed demands. This module suggests questions which need to be addressed by the practice that wishes to deliver high standards of service to its clients.

Our questions concerning client service follow the format of the current National Standards for Customer Service, established by representatives of industries who have already learnt that service is vital. Good service, leading to referrals and repeat business is, we suggest, the most effective marketing strategy a firm can have. Our final two questions then complement the first five by asking how well the practice knows its market and how carefully it has analysed its marketing activity.

2.1 How reliable are your standards of client service? How do you know?

- What records do you have regarding each client's needs and requirements?

- How does the design of your organisation help you to respond to changes in clients' needs?

- How can you establish whether people work together to deliver better service?

- How do you judge whether all partners and staff are fully committed, in practice, to delivering effective client service?

- How do you know whether the service you provide is consistent?

- What criteria do you use to assess whether all departments/business units provide the same consistent standards of service?

2.2 How good is your communication with clients?

- When did you last check your documentation, for example brochures or letters, to see if it is still relevant to clients?

- Do clients understand the language used by your practice?

- How do you get information back from clients? When did you last seek a new way of doing so?

- How sensitive are you to clients' time pressures?

- How skilled are your staff at adapting their communication method and style to the individual client?

- How could your working processes and systems be made more simple and client friendly?

2.3 How do you judge the success of your working relationships with clients?

- How often do you ask yourself whether clients' needs and feelings are identified and considered?

- Do you adapt your behaviour to suit?

- What standards of courtesy, accessibility and speed of response do you have and maintain?

- When a client's request does not seem possible how much effort do people in the practice put into exploring ways of meeting the request?

- If the request cannot be satisfied, how do you explain why not?

- What is your success rate at retaining clients?

- How often do existing clients recommend you to new clients?

- What records do you keep of 'occasional clients'?

- What systems do you have to remind them that you exist?

2.4 What effort do you put into understanding the client's perspective?

- When was the last occasion that you asked yourself what the real problem appeared to be from a client's perspective?

- How do you judge how proactive you are?

- When was the last time someone found a way of improving service?

- If you cannot meet a client's needs will you recommend them to a practice that you know can?

- How do you vet those to whom you will recommend clients?

- How do you monitor the client's perception of the value of your services and the value for money that you deliver?

2.5 How often do you look for ways to change in response to feedback from clients?

- How often do you seek and obtain feedback from clients?

- Who is able to suggest improvements in service?

- Are complaints encouraged and taken as opportunities for corrective action?

- Who is able to implement improvements?

- Are staff encouraged to treat clients as they would like to be treated? How do you know?

- Have you tried to monitor the impact of staff morale on client service?

- When did you last look at the image a client has of you from their point of view (your switchboard or reception may be their first point of call)?

2.6 What formal or informal market research do you have to tell you the demand for your particular services?

- What relevant data do you need on your markets?

- How is your business planning adjusted according to market data?

- How often do you compare your performance in particular markets with that of your competitors?

- When did you last review your marketing activities to ensure that they are focused and aligned with your practice strategy?

2.7 How do you market your business?

- Which possible marketing options have you considered?

- How do you analyse which succeed and which fail? What about ones you have not thought of?

- How do you know whether your various marketing ideas are working?

- Do you have a marketing plan with targets, objectives, budgets and alternatives?

- Have you assessed the time and money you spend on marketing against the amount of business you expect to generate:
  - generally
  - from new clients, and
  - from existing clients?

2.8 How well do you manage relationships with your key clients?

- How often do you 'audit' and 'value' your client relationships?

- Do you have an explicit process for identifying, monitoring and reviewing key client relationships?

- How do you identify and develop the skills of your client partners and client service teams?

- What processes and technologies do you have to enable you to share know-how about your clients?

- How well do you really know your client's business?

Practical Application Case Study:
Client Relationship Management (CRM)

- *Why are increasing numbers of firms focusing their attention on their 'key clients'?*

- *Why is gaining feedback from these clients so important?*

- *How do you demonstrate a real understanding of the business issues facing these clients?*

- *Why has a structured approach to CRM become one of the fastest growing processes introduced into the majority of medium and large firms?*

The vast majority of large practices have well developed CRM processes. Increasingly, the challenge is now falling upon the smaller and medium-sized practices to create more structured processes to what has often been an ad hoc and intuitive activity.

Client B is a medium-sized firm with some 20 plus partners and over 100 staff. They had experienced significant growth over a relatively short ten-year period. Much of the growth had been around some very strong relationships with a relatively small number of clients. Among these were a small number of high profile brands. Using the guidelines as an analytical framework it became apparent, however, that the work for these high profile clients was relatively limited – to one or two services at most. It was also apparent that these clients had other needs, although it was unclear which other firms were satisfying these needs.

The founder, now in his late 50s, recognised that a dangerously high proportion of these relationships were also heavily dependant on his network. He was also concerned that in many cases no explicit and agreed 'client partner' existed for other critical relationships. Furthermore, whilst feedback from clients was gathered on an ongoing basis, to date, the firm had not conducted any form of independent client feedback survey.

To redress these perceived 'threats', a proactive CRM process was introduced into the firm. The approach initially involved an intensive and independent review of the firm's top 20 clients. Based on the feedback from this process, client partners and client service teams were identified for each key client and a targeted action plan was developed. In parallel, a detailed business analysis was undertaken of each of the top 20 using a range of public and private domain data. This data, together with a detailed mapping of the depth and breadth of the relationships with the client organisation, identified a range of new opportunities for relationship and business development. Finally, coaching support was provided to help the client partners conduct their own client review meeting.

The process of focusing on these top 20 clients has proven to be an enlightening process for the partners. Many identified new information about the client which was not previously known, new relationship links were developed, clearer tactical marketing was undertaken and many new business opportunities identified. Above all, the process helped bring alive discussions about the firm's strategic positioning – and also put the spotlight on a small number of very unprofitable relationships from which the firm subsequently withdrew.

Practice
Management
Guideline 3

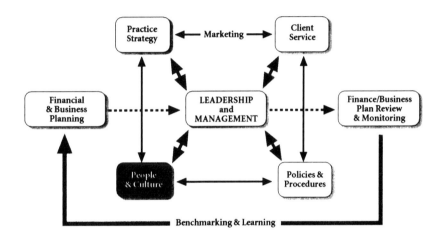

People and
Culture

*How well do you
know yourself and
lead others?*

Background Principles Guideline 3: People and Culture

Who would you rather employ, someone who wants to be part of the practice because it is their first choice or someone who is there because they do not, at the moment, have an alternative?

The terms 'professional' implies mastery of a particular body of knowledge, often involving representation through a professional body. It also usually signifies a range of common values, attitudes and behaviour:

- **Expertise, authority** and **status** flowing from expert and highly valued knowledge, understanding and skill – the ultimate arbiter of authority may, however, be the clients perception of the practice.

- The establishment of **exercise of trust** as a basis for professional relationships (with clients and between professionals).

- Adherence to particular **standards** and professional **ethics** often, but not always, represented by the granting of a licence to practice.

- Independence, **autonomy** and discretion.

- Specific attitudes towards work, clients and peers involving **reliability**, **flexibility** and **creativity** in relation to the 'unknown'.

The characteristics highlighted above have a number of consequences for the leader of a group of professionals. They demand that the exercise of authority flows through a process of influence and negotiation rather than by reliance on more direct position-based power. Individualistic professional activities can lead to stronger external relationships with clients being formed than with fellow professionals within the firm. Enabling horizontal communication links between apparently independent cells of professionals becomes a key leadership function. Indeed, the essence of managing professionals is creating a direction and an environment in which they can perform rather than relying solely on dictating the level of expected performance.

All 'equity partners' will wish to exert authority over decision making at least until such time as a less collegial decision-making structure is established and probably after that. The inevitable leadership challenge exists when the personal interests of the owners do not coincide with those charged with management decision making. Leadership is therefore, to a much greater extent, a responsibility of a wider group of individuals than in many more corporate environments. Without thinking about it perhaps, those who are effective in the process of leadership will be involved not only in providing direction but also in such interpersonal processes as:

- *Interpreting* – understanding the meanings behind people's words and clarifying that others understand them.

- *Negotiating* – building often unwritten and implicit agreements between individuals.

- *Networking* – creating formal and informal links within the firm and in the wider business world.

- *'Framing'* – influencing the frames of reference with which individuals make judgements of situations.

- *Signalling* – challenging, guiding and wielding influence.

Leadership is about making 'it' happen, deciding and articulating what 'it' is, and taking people with you individually and corporately. As the Chinese scholar Lao Tze wrote 3,000 years ago:

> 'Some leaders the people fear, others the people admire, the best they do not notice when the best leaders work is done the people say we did it ourselves.'

He remains one of the most frequently repeated theorists of all time. Since then, many historians, military tacticians and political theorists have joined the fray. In the 20th century, leadership has become a subject for academic research, mainly in the fields of psychology, politics and organisational behaviour. Approaches to the subject have developed into different schools of thought, each of which has provided useful insights for practical application. Some believe leaders are born not made. Others focus on the actions of leaders, integrating tasks, teams and individuals or on the circumstance in which different styles are appropriate. They focus on questions such as:

- The *quality of relationships* within a group: How good are they? Is there an appropriate balance between harmony and creative conflict?

- The *nature of the task*, particularly its degree of structure: How much ambiguity is there or how many dilemmas need to be resolved Is the task routine and predictable or is it messy and unclear?

- The *characteristics of group members* in terms of abilities, qualities and motivation: How willing and able are staff? What roles do they take on in groups? What motivates them at work or more broadly?

- The *position of the leader*, particularly in relation to power: How was the leader selected? What is the structure of group roles and tasks? What are the expectations of clients, staff, colleagues about the leadership role?

- *Time*: How urgent is the task? At what stage of development is the organisation?

- The *decision making process*: What is the balance of control over decisions between the leader and others, for example colleagues, clients? How significant is the decision at this point?

And finally:

- *Culture*: How do prevailing habits, beliefs and attitudes affect leadership, either locally within organisations, or across organisations and countries?

- *Context*: Is the leader leading business as usual or seeking a transformation to a different way of doing business?

Symbolism and culture – 'managing meaning'

Developing out of studies of leadership style, behaviour and influence in different settings and circumstances comes the idea that leadership is part of the belief systems which create frameworks and meanings for our working lives. Firms have been compared to tribes or nations drawn together by their particular rituals, myths, rites of passage and hierarchies.

The ways in which communication takes place in the office, the language that is used, the layout of office space, the marketing messages, the social interactions of the firm and the way promotions are handled and status granted, enable and constrain the firm's performance. They provide not only important clues about the organisation's values and culture, but also highlight the ways in which leadership is exercised. They all contribute to what Scott-Morgan (1996) called the 'unwritten rules of the game'. The culture of the firm and the results that it engenders are the result of this interplay. A leader can make things happen by thinking about what is happening and, if necessary, designing an environment where people feel free, or are even encouraged, to behave differently.

More practically, what do you as practice leader need to do? If leading professionals is about 'herding cats', what style and tactics should you adopt? What types of 'cat' do you have in your team and how do you create the conditions within which they are likely to be self-motivated.

Know your cats

The wise leader knows its cats. Teaching old cats (or, for that matter, young kittens) to perform new tricks can be very difficult. Playing to their strengths might be a better ploy. To help you identify your 'cats' and their strengths (and limitations), we have created eight hypothetical types of cat you might encounter in your practice.

- *Solo cat – the loner who walks by itself*
  Many professionals, especially those working in highly specialised or technological areas, are prone to being solo workers – getting on with the job their way. They work for the stimulation of using and developing their professional skills and relish the time to develop their new ideas, their way. It is an easy temptation to ask them to be involved in wider departmental activities; perhaps leading some specialist group or committee but it rarely pays off. Give the solo cat a clear idea of what is wanted and clear boundaries beyond which it cannot stray. Within these, more is perhaps gained by encouraging it to develop and mentor others than by expecting it to conform to a collective way of doing things.

- *Top cat – the entrepreneur who wants to drive every deal*
  Get some people engaged with a new idea and they will be off developing it in directions you never thought of. Ask them to work with someone else's idea and it's a different story. Entrepreneurs love the thrill of the new deal and the sense that they are taking a risk. The challenge may be to stop them from going so far, so fast, that they fail to realise how many people are not keeping up. These are the people who are motivated by status symbols and titles. They respond to accountability and responsibility but may need that accountability clearly defined before they go too far.

- *Aristo-cat – the traditionalist for whom the old ways are not only still best but still the only way.*

  'That's not how we did it in my day' 'Not a professional job' 'Standards are falling'. The traditionalist, or professional purist, poses one of the greatest leadership dilemmas. He may be a custodian of many of the firm's valued skills but time is passing him by and clients fade away. New incentives, new responsibilities can help remotivate such a person but the leader frequently has to spend time in one-to-one coaching, inviting and challenging the aristo-cat to see the world differently. You cannot change them. You can only encourage them to change themselves. Sometimes a complete shift to a different environment helps.

- *Plain old puss – reliable and friendly: but passed over for promotion and lacking apparent motivation to change his ways*

  Consultants who have let time pass by, and are either content to lie by the fire, or are disillusioned and withdrawn, need to feel valued if they are to deliver value. Unfortunately, they may have risen to their level of incompetence; then stopped. Honesty is the only answer. If possible play to their strengths and encourage them to work in a different way, perhaps as (again mixing metaphors) wise old owls alongside a rising young star. If they are also honest, it is at least possible.

- *The grand old cat – great in its day but living on the memory and reputation of past glories*

  Whereas a plain old puss may find it a relief to know its limits, stars from another era living on past glories can be a greater challenge. If you need them to remain motivated they tend to require ever-greater doses of ego massaging and peer recognition. Their great value is in the 'chair of our executive committee' role. Let them deal with those often value-detracting tasks that other departments, or other organisations throw at you.

- *The Number 10 cat – the consummate politician, usually on the look out for Number 1*

  Political animals just love networking and intriguing, sometimes for their own imagined gain and sometimes for the sheer pleasure of it. You want them doing it where it earns the firm a reputation with your clients rather than inside. Create the opportunity for them to play games and use their real skills where it won't do any real damage.

- *The cat who 'always lands on its feet' – difficult to pin down and make accountable*

  Whilst all cats are generally sure-footed some have the uncanny knack of avoiding any sense of failure and always land on their feet. These are the 'teflon types', nothing sticks, difficult to pin down and make accountable when things go wrong. Bide your time. You'll need to be patient and painstaking if you are to play on their pitch. Use their knowledge of systems and rules to your benefit. They know all the loopholes and dodges; involve them in reviewing procedures and contracts. Poachers turned gamekeepers can be useful allies.

- *The cat with attitude – has an opinion on everything and is always right – in its eyes anyway*

  Some people have a compulsion to look good and be right, to the point of being righteous. When you want someone to stone wall in the firm's interests outside it is wonderful. When you want the orchestra to play to a different tune it is a pain. Feed their obsession when it doesn't matter and there is more chance they will listen to you when it does.

At different times you want all these people in your team. Many research projects into team performance have established that great teams succeed in using and respecting different styles of working at different stages of the task in hand. There are any number of psychometric profiles available from quick self-assessments to expensive computer generated profiles. None has established an overarching reputation, despite the claims of their advocates to the contrary. What many of them can do is to give the leader an insight into different personalities and styles of operating. A team that uses one such tool together can get a collective insight into each other's personality and the styles of communication that are likely to work best for a given individual and situation.

Scott-Morgan, P. (1996) *The Unwritten Rules of the Game* Blackwell, Oxford

Guideline 3: How well do you know yourself and lead others?

The first two guidelines looked at **Strategy** deciding what you want to do, **Client Service** checking whether the practice is doing the right things and how well and **Marketing** satisfying the need for and creating a demand for such services. The leader's role is to make that strategy happen, or enable it by creating the environment in which it happens. Do you have a 'culture' or business environment in which people are motivated to deliver the forms of service that will accomplish the strategic goals of the practice?

Practices employ independent professionals: people who may even be more skilled in certain aspects of the job than those who 'manage' them. To lead such people it is not enough to simply be in charge, or to be 'the final expert' whose job is essentially professional quality control. Managers of professionals may perform both functions but they also have to inspire, or incentivise, or cajole, or ... these independent professionals to work together to achieve a common purpose. It is, as others have said before, like herding cats.

This guideline has seven elements. First is self-awareness and personal development. The leader who is aware of, and able to make allowance for, his or her own personal attributes is more likely to be able to accomplish the second element, understanding others and building effective relationships. Without such understanding it is unlikely that the leader can provide either a shared sense of purpose or develop a set of reward systems that lead to the achievement of the overall purpose. Reviewing performance objectively requires clear objectives. Self and peer understanding are also the foundation for understanding the 'informal' myriad of subtle interactions which can govern many aspects of behaviour within the practice. A further characteristic of practice leaders is, we suggest, the ability to develop others and above all to stimulate change; to keep the practice responsive to its changing environment.

3.1   How well do you know and develop yourself?

- How well do you know your personal aspirations from the practice? What are they?

- How well do you understand your preferred style of operating at work? What is it?

- How easy do you find it to question your assumptions about people and their actions?

- How easy do you find it to question your assumptions about business issues or problems?

- What personal targets have you set for your own continued development of self-awareness and interpersonal skills?

- When you decide on a course of action, how committed are you to taking personal responsibility for making it happen?

- How do you ensure your management actions set the example you would like to be followed?

3.2 How clearly do you understand others and the process of building effective business relationships?

- How well do you understand the aspirations of others, especially your clients, partners and employees?

- Do you fully understand what creates a sense of self-motivation in your fellow partners? What do you think they want to be famous for?

- What gets your employees out of bed in the morning and motivates them to work for you?

- How do you modify your style of operating and communicating to suit the needs of a particular task or to relate to others?

- How easy do you find it to listen to others and explore their point of view when the circumstances dictate?

- How easy do you find it to clarify and communicate your own point of view?

- How do you assess the level of diversity which is appropriate for the practice?

- How do you harness the diversity?

3.3 What shared 'sense of direction' do you provide?

- What shared sense of direction and common purpose have you established for the partners and the practice?

- Over what time-scale does the vision extend?

- How much involvement of other partners, or of staff, went into creating that vision?

- How do you check the degree to which the vision is shared by others in the practice?

- What actions do you take to communicate, maintain and reinforce the vision?

- How do you know the practice is 'on track'?

3.4 What formal and informal performance review and reward systems exist?

- What formal systems exist for assessing people's performance and aspirations?

- How do you clarify the specific goals/challenges/objectives for your fellow partners and staff?

- What actions and behaviours get rewarded in the practice? Are rewards based solely on seniority or are they related to all aspects of job performance?

- Does your reward system reinforce your practice strategy and encourage co-operation as opposed to competition between groups?

- How do you deal with under performers and those who 'don't fit'?

3.5 Do you understand the 'culture' and 'unwritten rules' of the practice?

- How would you characterise the culture of your practice?

- Have you considered whether it needs to change? If so, in what ways?

- What are the 'unwritten' rules which exist within the practice and which govern behaviour? Do some of these inhibit performance?

- If you could write the 'Ten Commandments' for the practice, what would they be? How do they compare with reality?

3.6 What amount of time and effort do you spend on the development of others?

- How do you identify what capabilities and skills you will need in the practice for the future?

- How do you establish the needs of individuals for growth and development?

- How do you translate these needs into your succession planning processes?

- What proportion of your time do you devote to the coaching of your team members?

- How do you balance the needs of individual professionals for freedom and challenge with those of direction, constraints and constructive feedback?

3.7 How well do you stimulate changes to aspects of the practice's operation?

- What mechanisms do you have in place for assessing the need for change. If you need to change how will you make it happen?

- How much time do you spend reviewing whether the practice's plans and strategies are still appropriate to its current business environment?

- What are your current priorities for improving the practice's business?

- How do you encourage the practice, and everyone in it, to continually or periodically question ways of doing things: in essence are they involved in a process, formal or informal, of continuous improvement?

- What example do you set when it comes to continual improvement and development?

Practical Application Case Study: People and Culture

Client C is a medium-sized firm operating nationally and internationally. As part of a development programme for the Board each member had been given the opportunity to select an executive coach to work with them to further enhance and develop their leadership style and approach. Over a period of 18 months (meeting typically for 1.5 hours every four to six weeks) we explored a number of dimensions of Colin's (not his real name) approach to leadership.

Colin was a well respected and highly competent professional and seemed to be well liked by staff in his department (around 30).

Using the guidelines, we began by exploring how Colin perceived his approach to leadership – and agreed to a 360 degree review. In essence, this involved the use of a structured questionnaire to invite (in a non-attributable and confidential manner) a group of peers and team members to provide feedback on Colin's approach to leadership. Using such a tool requires careful handling, as does the feedback and interpretation.

The feedback from the exercise re-emphasised the considerable respect with which Colin was held. He had strengths as a coach to his junior colleagues, he delegated well and he operated an 'open door' policy – and unlike some others who professed to this approach, he was generally available. Inevitably, Colin also gained insight into areas of development – some of his peers felt that a clearer sense of direction was required, that more communication would be beneficial and that a less ad hoc approach to planning was required. On the behavioural side he gained further insights – that he should consider dealing with interpersonal conflict between team members more directly, that on occasions he should be more directive in his style … and so on.

Having identified a personal action plan, our coaching sessions then focused on implementation. The emphasis throughout was to ensure we play to Colin's strengths, whilst also tackling some of his development needs. The planning and communication issues were relatively easy to identify – although progress took longer than originally anticipated. On the behavioural side, the sessions focused on real life interpersonal issues and an opportunity to practise, in a 'safe' environment, the approaches required to deal with a number of difficult personnel issues.

Over time, the focus changed to address the cultural barriers to progress – in particular, the nature of 'the unwritten rules' which required discussion if the existing culture was to be modified.

By the end of the process, Colin felt he had gained considerable self-insight and had developed a wider repertoire of leadership styles. He also felt he now understood better why he was successful in many of the approaches he adopted – and had a better appreciation of his blind spots.

Practice
Management
Guideline 4

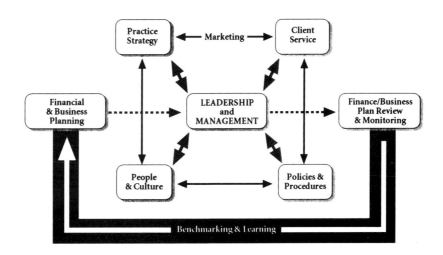

Learning through Benchmarking, Training and Development

How do you compare the practice's performance?

Background Principles: Guideline 4 Learning through Benchmarking, Training and Development

'You don't have to do this [change and improve]: survival is not compulsory'

(W Edwards Demming)

'The ability to learn is the only sustainable source of competitive advantage'

(A de Geus)

When we started work on these guidelines, Benchmarking, Learning, Training and Development were four words that cropped up in various guises as the latest 'miracle cures' for continued business performance; four more fads thrust upon the modern professional in a plethora of initiatives, advertisements, standards, questionnaires and consultants sales literature. Today, they have been joined, or surpassed, by 'knowledge management'. What do they mean for the busy managing partner?

First, does anything distinguish training, development and the elusive 'learning'?

One answer is 'time-scale'. Training tends to be short-term and relatively discontinuous. We go or send someone on a course when we perceive we, or they, need to know something, or even when they have a problem. Development may imply a more continuous process, a reflection of ongoing acquisition of new skills and experience.

Another may be 'who is responsible'. We go or send our staff to trainers out of the assumption that they are 'experts' with answers. Repeat the formula and maybe if you do, you too will be able to do it. Learning is perhaps more personal. We acquire new skills or ideas or ways of doing things when we discover them for ourselves. Teachers (or coaches or facilitators) can help that process of individual discovery. Managers may decide to buy training for their staff. Leaders perhaps take more responsibility for facilitating the learning of their people.

A third may be the process involved. Training can be restricted to acquisition of knowledge; a 'know what' process. Development can imply more emphasis on skills acquired over time; a 'know how' process. For some, learning has a deeper meaning, associated with understanding; a 'know-why' process. As we 'learn' we may first have to discard or suspend older habits and opinions. We do not learn to walk out of the comfortable habits of crawling or ride bicycles out of the intuitive balancing that goes into walking.

The comparison is not unlike the challenge facing the professional of the future. As we have observed already in this series, the world is changing from the days when the client purchased answers from experts to one in which they expect professionals to work with them on developing joint solutions. Even in the supposed high ground of independent valuation, the foundation of many a surveying practice, research is challenging the validity of that underlying premise of independent, objective, expertise.

Most of the evidence of modern research into organisations is that the 'learning' approach works better. In the long term it generates healthier – and more financially successful – companies. The old way is, however, deeply ingrained. We are accustomed to seek 'instant answers'. When they work it is fine, and there are many cases where training is appropriate and necessary. However, continuing the theme of the feline orchestra, one can train dogs or herd sheep, but cats make up their own minds.

These 'guidelines' are designed around a learning approach. We are more concerned to help the user find their own way to develop a better practice than to offer instant cures for problems the practice may or may not suffer.

Benchmarking is surveying's legacy to 'management speak'! The term comes from the profession and the first recorded 'bench-marks' are inscribed on the pyramids. Whether Egyptian management practice treated those people as surveyors, architects or project managers is not known: perhaps professional multi-skilling is also an old invention. In modern managerial usage, benchmarking refers to the study and emulation (or learning from) of best ways of doing something, in or outside one's industry. Unlike other forms of competitive performance assessment, it is an open and essentially collaborative process and one that, used to full advantage, involves much more than merely compiling league tables of comparative data. At heart, it is one process by which a firm can discover for itself new ways of operating (if it is prepared to loosen its attachment to the old ones).

For the professional firm Practice Learning is the sum of all or part of the individual learning achieved by the members of the firm. Traditionally, CPD has been taken, for the professional at least, as the measure of that learning. That emphasis is changing.

From	To
Counting CPD Inputs: the hours of course attended	Considering CPD Outputs: the results, knowledge and skills achieved
An emphasis on formal training	An equal empahsis on informal learning
An emphasis on the development of professional skills	An emphasis on professional, interpersonal and managerial skills
An emphasis on recording CPD	An emphasis on planning and structuring learning

'Sustainable business success is not just about intelligent individuals – it is about intelligent organisations which are capable of learning.' (RSA Inquiry 1995:17)

What then determines whether or not development helps a particular practice. In our experience the following are critical:

1   Think of an active learning process rather than a training process. Staff at whatever level who feel they are motivated and encouraged to develop respond better than staff who are told they need to be trained.

2 Think from the perspective of the business result you want to achieve. People working towards something that is on the leadership agenda are more enthusiastically supported than those who are 'doing something in their spare time'.

3 The firm's learning plan flows from the firm's business plans and business challenges.

4 Find providers of training and assistance who can work with you to establish a flexible process that delivers results for the firm and recognition for your staff.

5 Use standards as benchmarks which people and the business will meet in their own way, not as prescriptive lists of 'how to do it' as well as 'what to do'.

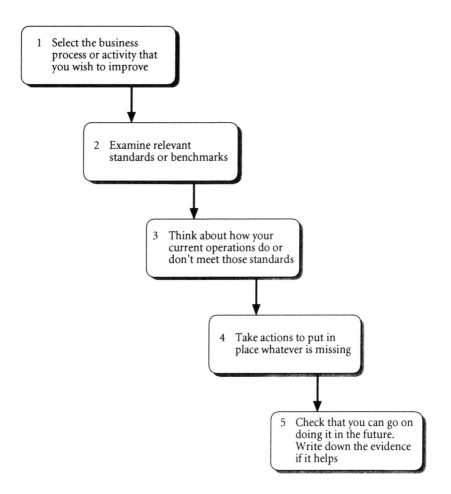

1 Select the business process or activity that you wish to improve

2 Examine relevant standards or benchmarks

3 Think about how your current operations do or don't meet those standards

4 Take actions to put in place whatever is missing

5 Check that you can go on doing it in the future. Write down the evidence if it helps

Guideline 4: How do you compare the practice's performance and develop its capabilities?

Learning carries many different meanings. We use it to refer to the ability of a practice – or any organisation – to adapt to, and if necessary lead, changes in its environment. To do so the individuals in the practice, at all levels, must themselves learn; a process which demands developing and changing the mental models through which they interpret the world. Training may be part of the learning process, as may continued development of professional knowledge and skills. Here we seek to stimulate continued learning in other aspects of the practice such as its position vis-à-vis competitors, its ways of organising its business operations and, perhaps most importantly of all, its ways of approaching people and interpersonal skills.

Our first question concerns benchmarking and other methods of comparing oneself to competitors or collaborators. Leading organisations in many sectors of business are discovering the paradox that another organisation can, in today's business environment, be both competitor and collaborator. Continually watching the outside world for inspiration and example is a prerequisite of continued success.

Secondly, whilst benchmarking in the strict sense involves other organisations, various professional and national standards for professional work – and also for management and service – can be seen as ready-made benchmarks against which to judge the practice's performance. Whilst imposed 'standards' have, rightly, met with negative reactions in many professional service organisations; standards used as benchmarks provide targets for future business development.

Building on that theme, the third question emphasises the need for training and development, and especially learning, to be part of the ongoing business plans of the practice. The knowledge thus gained will, for a service practice, be stored in the minds of each partner or employee and deployed in the way they do their jobs and relate to others, in and outside the practice.

Our fourth question, therefore, concerns the practice encouraging and supporting its people to develop themselves. Leaders who can act as coaches, facilitating the performance and learning of others, are a powerful and necessary enabler of that development.

The final question under this *Guideline* covers such coaching.

Appendix 1 is a summary of the national Investors In People (IIP) standards 'translated' into the style and language used in the other guidelines in this series. Whether or not a practice finds the formal IIP award a useful part of its business development, the standards offer a ready made guide to assessing the degree to which the practice supports a 'learning' culture.

4.1 Do you have formal or informal methods for benchmarking the practice's performance?

- How does the practice monitor the success of its business operations versus those of potential competitors?

- What formal or informal processes do you have in place for evaluating the performance of the practice relative to others?

- What formal or informal processes do you have in place for evaluating the operations of the practice compared with others, in similar or other markets?

- What do you regard as critical to the practice's success? On what basis do you judge the standards you achieve in these critical areas?

- How much encouragement is given to staff to experiment with different ways of operating?

4.2 Do you use existing 'standards' and guidelines as benchmarks?

- How do you decide what standards of performance are expected of people at various levels in the practice?

- How do you judge professional work against the relevant professional standards?

- How do you judge your standards for managerial and administrative procedures, for client service, or other business activities of the practice?

- Which of the following have you formally adopted or considered as an informal check on current activities:
  (a) Relevant professional standards?
  (b) ISO 9000/9001 or similar?
  (c) Investors In People?
  (d) National Vocational Standards?
  (e) Others?

- What targets has the practice set itself for incorporating standards of good practice into its work in the future?

- How familiar are you with the sources of assistance (financial and otherwise) regarding operational and development standards which are available to practices of your size.

4.3 How do you link training and development plans to business plans?

- Do your business plans include a review of the future skills and capabilities needed in the practice's employees?

- What data do you collect and review to support that analysis?

- What plans have you made to ensure that those skills are either recruited or developed? What options have you considered?

- In the plans you have made, what specific objectives, priorities and time-scales are set for individual development?

- Who is assigned roles and responsibilities for their achievement?

- How is the investment in skills development evaluated?

4.4 What do you do to encourage individual development?

- How many of the practice's employees do you regard as having a career in the practice? How many do you regard as having a job?

- Do you have a formal policy of developing a percentage of the practice's employees? What is it and how do you assess its success?

- How often do you formally, or informally, review people's development and aspirations?

- What personal development goals have you agreed with your staff?

- What percentage of partner time is devoted to helping others with their development?

- What financial resources are available in the practice to encourage individual development?

- What leadership examples are set for professional or personal development?

- When individuals or work groups acquire new skills or create new solutions to business problems, how do you celebrate and acknowledge their achievement?

- What formal or informal plans for people's career development in, or outside, the practice have you made with them?

- What is your attitude to:
  - (a) professional skill development
  - (b) managerial and business skills development, and
  - (c) support staff development?

  Is it:
  - (1) we hire people and expect them to be competent
  - (2) we send people on the relevant courses, or
  - (3) we see it as part of our job to encourage people to develop new skills?

4.5 Do you encourage partners to coach others in the practice?

- How well do you understand the individual goals and communication styles of your employees?

- What records do you maintain of those goals?

- How often, and in what ways, is progress towards those goals assessed?

- Do you formally recognise the value of developing skills through coaching?

- What opportunities to practise newly acquired skills do you create?

- When mistakes are made how do you handle them: by searching for someone to blame, or as an opportunity to learn?

- How do you make time more explicitly available for such informal learning?

Practical Application Case Study: Benchmarking and Learning

Client D is a highly successful and well established medium-sized practice. The firm had a long history and a strong client base. Its culture was dominated by a focus on tradition, although several of the younger partners felt it was 'old-fashioned' and increasingly 'out of touch' with the changes in the market. Over a period of three years, following the retirement of a number of the older equity partners, the firm refocused its strategy under a new leadership team.

By the time we were invited to meet with the new senior team, the firm's finances had improved considerably. However, the firm felt, based on anecdotal evidence, that they were less successful than other comparably sized firms. But to date they had no real indication of the extent of any under-performance or, indeed, whether a real gap existed.

Using the guidelines as a start point, we focused our attention on *Guideline 4*. The concept of benchmarking was familiar to the senior management. They had been invited to join a benchmarking club and indeed had submitted copious data to the independent agency conducting the exercise. By the time we met, a large document had been sitting on the managing partner's desk for a few days. The initial analysis indicated that on the vast majority of measures the firm was performing well – 4th (out of 15) in terms of profitability, 5th in terms of fee income/staff member, 5th on the ratio of income/£ of staff costs, and the lowest in terms of the percentage of costs spent on accommodation. So, what was the problem?

The problem, the astute managing partner identified, lay not in the results but how he could engage the partners and others in learning from the process and the results. Whilst much good news existed, the firm was 8th in terms of growth and not as effective in a number of other areas. He was also sceptical about some of the results – he was concerned that the positive results could lead to complacency – whereas he felt they needed to set themselves much more demanding targets.

We jointly agreed that the most effective way to deal with the issue was to facilitate an 'awayday' at which the results would be summarised and discussed. We all recognised that engaging and involving the partners in reviewing the data was crucial. We started by focusing on the positive results – and debated how these encouraging results could be enhanced even further. We then challenged the group to think beyond the confines of the results from the benchmarking club. We challenged the group by examining results from a range of other professional service firms – law firms, consultancy practices and accountants. The results of the top performers in these sectors were in a number of areas very much higher than those for the surveying practices. Why? What do they do that we don't? What can we learn from these results? We also asked the group to consider which other high performing surveying firms had not been included in the results.

We subsequently focused on the areas where the results had been less positive. What could we learn from others – how had the best performers in each of the key ratios achieved these results? And, of course, we also had to try and second guess who the (anonymous) top performing firms were.

By the end of the day a practical action plan had been developed to focus on the areas which would be of most benefit in terms of enhancing the financial performance of the firm. A new client management programme was established, a new balanced scorecard of performance measures was agreed and a revised business planning process was initiated.

Practice
Management
Guideline 5

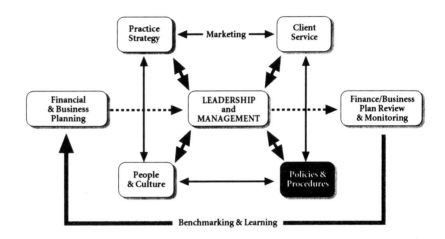

Policies and
Procedures

*How can they
add value to
the practice?*

Background Principles: Guideline 5 Policies and Procedures

Who needs a policy?

A common problem faces many small and start-up businesses. In the pressure and financial uncertainty of securing their niche, they fail to invest in developing the systems, capacity, capability or processes that they will need as their business grows. Suddenly, growth dramatically slows or reverses as the partners, busy with fighting fires, cannot develop new business. The problem is spotting what will be the next limit before it impacts on the business.

Many limits crop up. Growth may be constrained by capacity, or staff, or lack of time and effort on marketing, or lack of attention to service quality. Less glamorous than many of these, but equally critical, is the humble policy statement (and the actions that stem from it).

There are many areas where policy may not be necessary. There are equally many reasons for deciding whether to have a policy. Some firms, for example, make their staff development policies, or their service quality policies, a fundamental part of the unique selling proposition they present to their clients.

In the modern economy, firms ultimately depend on public goodwill, or on the licence to operate. Loss of reputation with customers, the local community, or staff, damages the cash flow. So called 'Corporate Social Responsibility', an ethical stance and policy on employment issues, community and environmental issues, makes – to a point that they have to judge – good business sense.

Established ways of doing things can enable people to operate within their own initiative without having to demand the time and attention of partners or other income generators on trivial issues. Is it really necessary to give personal attention to everything that is clogging up the in-tray?

It may be *legally* necessary, for example, in areas of **health and safety** or **employment regulations**.

The topic of policies and procedures is the necessary evil or bane of existence for most practices. However, it is worth reviewing them occasionally, if only to check that just the necessary is retained and the remainder is eliminated. Apparently, it was only in 1955 that the British Army finally removed the post whose job was to stand on the White Cliffs of Dover and ring a bell in the case of a French invasion.

Guideline 5: When did you last review your operating procedures and policies?

For want of a nail the shoe was lost
For want of a shoe the horse was lost
For want of a horse the rider was lost
For want of a rider the message was lost
For want of a message the battle was lost
For want of a battle the war was lost
For want of the war the nation was lost.

Unglamorous, boring even, the topic of policies and procedures; the necessary evil or bane of existence for most professionals. However, we can categorise them as follows:

- Some policies and procedures are necessary. They are part of the requirements of staying in business.

- Some policies and procedures are also useful. They save you money in a variety of ways.

- Some policies and procedures are even strategic. They form part of the special mix of capabilities that distinguishes your practice from its competitors.

Practices, as they grow, face an extended list of legal obligations; requirements that they must comply with. Non-compliance carries business risk, up to and including the risk of being barred from future trading, but compliance does not in itself guarantee success. Strategic differentiation comes from the practice's distinctive capabilities, embedded in the way it does things. In this section, we suggest distinguishing policies – formal statements that are adopted to ensure regulatory compliance – from procedures – the formal or in some cases more informal ways a practice has of doing things. You may have no policies. You will have procedures, even if they are informal. There comes a time when it is worthwhile for an expanding practice to write down how it does what it does, if only as a way of checking whether it is doing something that is unnecessary.

These questions aim to help partners decide which policies and procedures fall into which category and this stage of the practice's development. Have you:

- Reviewed which fall into which category?

- Taken the necessary actions to ensure any new policies and procedures are implemented?

- Checked that you do not have any old policies and procedures, appropriate to past business, still operating?

The operation of formal, or informal, quality assurance system is a topic likely to exercise the mind of many partners. Some practices have found registration for the international quality standard – ISO 9000 – to be a benefit. Others have found it unnecessary or even unhelpful. Readers who want details are referred to the RICS document 'Quality Assurance for the Interpretation of ISO 9000 for use by Chartered Surveyors and Quality Assurance Bodies, 2nd Edition 1996'.

5.1 Do you periodically review the needs of the practice for policies and procedures?

- When did the practice last review the policies and procedures it has and consider whether they are needed?

- What percentage of staff had their opinions considered during that review?

- How were clients' requirements taken into account during that review?

- What sources of external expertise did you consider necessary?

- Which of the following reviews did you undertake to quantify the benefits to the practice of existing policies and procedures:

- What are the legal risks of not having adequate policies and procedures?

  - What is the likelihood of lost business as a result of inadequate policies and procedures?

  - How much time and other resources are wasted through not having good policies and procedures?

  - What are the strategic benefits of certain policies and procedures?

5.2 How regularly do you design and implement policies and procedures that meet the needs of the practice?

- In designing new policies and procedures, or reviewing existing ones, are you aware of the current legal and regulatory requirements?

- Are new policies and procedures planned to meet future operational priorities at a realistic cost? How do you know?

- When deciding to implement a new policy or procedure, on what timescale do you expect it to be needed (ie how far ahead does the practice find it desirable/necessary to look)?

5.3 Do you periodically evaluate the effectiveness of existing policies and procedures and identify opportunities for improvement?

- When did you last obtain feedback from staff, or clients if relevant, on how well critical policies and procedures are operating?

- When did you last consider what they are costing and whether there is a return on the investment?

- When did you last seek to improve the operation of existing policies and procedures?

- Are improvements to operating policies and procedures part of the practice's forward business plan?

Practical Application Case Study: Policies and Procedures

Client E is the London office of a larger practice which trades quite independently in another part of the country. For historical reasons, the firm was constituted as two separate partnerships although both traded under a single brand name. A collective partnership agreement bound both of the partnerships together in a legal sense but, for all intents and purposes, the two businesses operated separately.

The initial brief for the client was to work with the partners of the London partnership to assist with a strategic review of the existing business and identify specific actions to help grow the business in the medium term.

The *Guidelines* proved to be a helpful catalyst for debate around the strategic challenges facing the business. However, it became clear that one of the areas where considerable potential existed for enhanced profitability was in relation to the processes, systems and procedures used by both parts of the firm. Despite a common letterhead, the firms gained very little synergy from their collective relationship. Part of the story, as is so often the case, related to a lack of trust between the partners – although much of the acrimony has now passed.

It was therefore agreed that, with the intention of building common ground and mutual understanding, an audit of current processes and systems would be undertaken in order to assess where gains could be made through shared infrastructure and approaches.

The outcome was a list of agreed changes to the firm's administrative systems (particularly in relation to finance and personnel) and an agreement to share market knowledge and client data in a much more transparent manner.

Over time, the gains from the process also helped build trust between the two separate groups. This ultimately led to both partnerships investing in a new jointly owned office and, in time, to a restructuring of the business with a single partnership agreement.

Practice
Management
Guideline 6

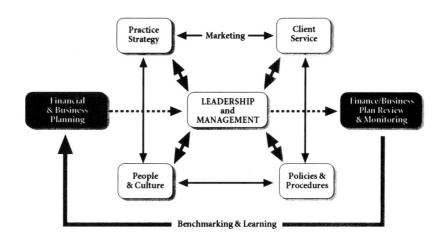

Practice Finance

*How can you
improve
profitability?*

Background Principles: Guideline 6 Practice Finance

Keeping a professional firm in a happy state of high long-term profitability is theoretically simple. Sell as much time of your fee-earning staff as possible, at the highest possible price. Keep costs as low as possible while adequately resourcing the business and ensuring its long-term health. Bill promptly while persuading clients to pay quickly and keep an eye on the vagaries of cash flow.

However, those who manage firms know that the story is not so simple. Every firm has particular challenges it has to meet to improve its financial performance and the ease with which that performance can be managed. This section identifies the typical financial and related management challenges which firms typically face. These are categorised as:

- Plan
- Optimise structure
- Manage and control
- Monitor performance
- Control costs
- Price right
- Manage cash flow
- Manage partners' investment and return.

Plan

The only things which can be confidently said about the future, are that it is uncertain, although we have some idea of where we are now. To grope blindly into the gloom with no sense of direction and with no alternative routes planned if our road proves impassable, does little to ensure survival. Planning is all.

What state do we want the firm to be in, three to five years hence? Within that framework, how should we set out to manage and resource our practice over the coming year? What are our operational plans for each fee-earning unit and central function?

From a financial point of view, we then need to cost these plans for the future, have some prediction of probable revenue and identify our consequent funding requirements.

Optimise structure

The shape we decide for the practice decides our income-generating potential and operational costs. We have choices, too, in deciding whether we will own or lease the infrastructure of the business – our premises and equipment. All this, plus the manner by which we choose to regulate our financial relationship with clients, will determine the funding requirements of the business.

However we choose to fund the firm, through partners' equity, retained profit or debt, we need also to ensure that funds can easily be accessed if we hit a period of negative cash flow.

Manage and control

A challenge for any firm, is that of creating a systematic approach to the management of financial performance. This requires that the partnership delegates true control to nominees; that authorities and responsibilities are clearly understood and owned by everyone who has a role in financial management, at firm, department or individual client level.

Ownership further requires a preparedness to manage; for example, to prune a practice of unprofitable areas of activity, clients or individual fee earners, if no cost-effective way of increasing their yield can be found.

All this also entails the further challenge that all who manage and control any aspect of performance must have a sufficient understanding of the components of profitability. Progressive development of appropriate financial understanding needs to occur at all levels of the practice.

Monitor performance

Enabling financial management also requires current performance information to be available. The challenge is to identify the Key Performance Indicators (KPIs) which will quickly and comprehensively tell us how well the business is running. All aspects of operation should be capable of measurement; including (and sometimes controversially) the performance of individual partners.

Fight the temptation to give those that manage, detail for the sake of detail. At the summary level, performance for a unit can be reported by just eight indicators:

- income against budget
- costs against budget
- average recovery against budget rate
  - write-offs
  - bad debts
- average utilisation
- average billing speed, and
- average collection speed.

Enable 'helicopter vision' by isolating these, but provide access to the explanatory detail.

Control costs

Professional firms are fixed-cost businesses. Profit is exponentially affected by small variations in activity, because as income fluctuates, costs remain almost unchanged.

Those managing an expanding firm have to consider carefully the level of support staff required to directly resource fee-earners, and the extent of staff central functions such as marketing, human resources, systems, and accounts. Once a cost structure is established, it is hard to dismantle. The challenge, is to keep the firm lean but adequately resourced to efficiently do business in the immediate future. The longer term development of the practice has to be funded too.

If there is a trend towards poorer performance, as in a recession, it is hard to maintain profitability by pushing costs down to match. Serious attempts at cost cutting are likely to involve dismantling part of the practice, losing past investment. Cost cutting can also involve short term cost increases through redundancy charges and lease surrender penalties.

Price right

One of the greatest challenges for professional firms is to price work at a level that maximises returns while maintaining competitiveness. Some services have their prices set by the marketplace or by a regulatory body. Other services give more latitude to firms to price for themselves. To establish the price for a service requires an appreciation of what the market can bear, allied with understanding of the resources required to complete the task and their cost.

In competitive tender situations, pricing requires sound comprehension of how discounting below desired price levels will affect profitability. This also requires appreciation of the risks and possible losses of the job.

Create the machinery to enable the resource planning and consequent costing of work. Enable measurement of the job cost of individual fee earners.

Manage cash flow

Most businesses that go bust, do so because they experience a period of adverse cash flow which they are unable to fund. Many are profitable businesses, generating a good margin. Despite this apparent health, a temporary embarrassment of poor income in a particular month, contrasted perhaps with higher than normal costs, could lead to failure or having to resort to expensive forms of debt or factoring.

Professional firms can be hit by low cash income during a period, through a seasonal down-cycle in trade or through tardy client payments. The situation cannot be easily remedied by delaying creditor payments, which are for the most part strategically important; the largest cash outgoing is usually on staff salaries.

In these circumstances, financial managers should have the authority to suspend or reduce partners' monthly drawings and even of penalising those who are failing to manage client payments well. Sound short-term debt arrangements must also be in place to create a cushion against the worst conceivable cash deficit.

Manage partners' investment and return

A final challenge for professional firms, is to ensure fair treatment for equity partners which brings in sufficient funding and gives individuals a return which reflects their personal contribution to fee earning and the management and development of the practice.

The exit route for retiring partners should fully reimburse their equity contribution and recognise their undrawn profits and contribution to the practice over the years.

Summary

Plan for the long term. Re-plan each year as a different future unfolds. Produce costed annual budgets and marketing plans.

Optimise the fee-earning and support staff structure of the practice. Enable high and balanced utilisation of fee-earning resources.

Enable real financial management of the business by creating authority, accountability and clear delegation of responsibility and tasks. Develop financial competence.

Monitor performance by recognising Key Performance Indicators. Create the systems to ensure their timely reporting.

Avoid unnecessary costs but don't waste management time saving pennies when there are pounds of fee income to be won.

Price right and restrict losses due to discounting, write-offs, and bad debts.

Manage cash flow, predicting future deficits to enable funding.

Manage partners' investment and return. If the owners of the business enable you and your team to manage it, with authority; in return they will expect good profit and an equitable means of distribution.

In introducing systematic financial planning, performance monitoring and control mechanisms into your firm, remember that it is a 'people' business. These mechanisms should enable good management, not stifle it.

Guideline 6: How can you increase your profits?

We have endeavoured to emphasise the practice as a total system. All aspects of its operations are linked. The final component will ensure that the system is making, and continues to make, a return commensurate with the efforts and ambitions of its partners or shareholders. We summarise managerial budgeting and accounting, pricing the services delivered, and the essential legal and fiscal requirements for continuing operation.

We assume most users of these *Guidelines* will be familiar with the major principles of management and financial accounting, profit and loss statements and balance sheets. We concentrate instead on the financial management responsibilities of the partners.

- Ensuring adequate plans and budgets exist for the practice.

- Monitoring actual trading to ensure adequate cash is available to the practice (a point of particular priority for the smaller practice).

- Monitoring actual trading to ensure the practice is maintaining adequate profitability.

- Adequate planning of the capital resources and investment.

- Improving financial performance, via cost control, fees and credit control and tax management.

We have included a section on succession planning as a financial issue. Some founders of a successful practice may consider the return on either their financial investment, or their time during the early days, comes in the money earned whilst they remain a partner. Many, however, have a significant stake in the practice in the form of either initial investments or reinvested profits. If a return on that investment is to be realised it is likely that existing partners will wish to sell equity to newer colleagues. Not all practices survive past the retirement of the founder or of the second generation of partners. Those that do, generally see the long term development of future partners as a process to be planned over some years.

6.1 How often do you plan the routine financial aspects of the practice?

- How are the financial objectives of the practice set out in the business plans?

- Do you have processes in place to determine your threshold of profitability in different areas of the practice?

- Over what period(s) do you calculate break-even points for the practice?

- Which areas of the practice do you calculate break-even points for?

- How accurate is your budgeting and forecasting?

- At what intervals are budgets and forecasts reviewed by the partners?

- Are you getting the advice you need from your accountant, bank manager or other appropriate specialists?

- Are forecasts, budgets and management accounting adequately integrated into a financial management system for the practice?

- How often do you review options for obtaining finance?

- Have you tested the sensitivity of your financial plans to changes in the main factors which might affect them?

6.2 Does the practice have an adequate cash flow to meet its projected future commitments?

- What sources of cash is the practice utilising?

- What cash flow objectives are specified in the practice's financial objectives?

- What methods do you use to control sources and uses of cash?

- How often do you do cash flow forecasts? Is this adequate?

- Where cash shortfalls occur, are they accurately forecasted?

- What action is planned, in the event of a cash shortfall, with appropriate financial sources?

6.3 Is this practice profitable?

- What profit objectives are specified in the financial strategy of the practice?

- How regularly do you assess the income and expenditure of the practice?

- How accurately can you assess the match between your profit objectives and your income and expenditure?

- Over what time-scale do you forecast profits? How reliably are you able to budget?

- What controls of income and expenditure are in place?

- Are legitimate ways of minimising tax identified and used?

- What profit margins are made on different services, or from different clients?

- How accurately can you apportion significant overhead costs to different areas of business?

6.4 What actions are taken to maintain and enhance performance?

Through performance measurement?

- What measures do you routinely use to assess how well the practice is performing?

- Do you examine performance by:

  - Particular areas of business (or offices)?

  - Particular sectors?

- Particular clients?
- Particular types of job (eg those charged on commission, versus a day rate)?

- Do your measures include:
  - Measures of profit against fees?
  - Measures of fee income against time?
  - Measures of billable time per person or partner?
  - Measure of people time billed per unit of partner time?
  - Measure of profit against capital employed?

- What actions have you taken to change operational decisions as a result of performance measurement?

Through cost control?

- What approval procedures for expenditure against budgets are in place?

- Are financial transactions accurately recorded and assigned to the correct accounts against your budget?

- How often are variances between budget and actual expenditure examined? What actions are taken?

- When preparing budgets do you periodically 'zero-base'; ie examine the necessity for the expenditure rather than project from previous years?

- How often do you review the costs of regular items purchased from your suppliers?

- What policies do you operate for paying your creditors?

Through effective monitoring of fee levels?

- On what basis do you calculate the fees charged for a particular job?

- How do you assess whether or not the charges are at the level that the market will bear?

- In calculating fees, and assigning overhead costs to particular jobs and tenders, do you take into account the consumption of different overhead costs by the contract concerned?

- How do you assess the possible impact on the practice of raising fees?

- How do you assess the possible impact on the practice of a more aggressive billing schedule?

Through efficient credit management?

- How do you assess the possible impact on the practice of a more aggressive credit control policy?

- How much was owed to the practice at the end of last month?

- How much of that was overdue for payment?

- What interest would the overdue money have earned, even in a simple deposit account?

- How is credit authorised?

- How often are accounts payable monitored and by whom?

- Is there a defined credit control policy in action?

- Are interim accounts rendered promptly?

6.5 Does the practice manage its relationship with providers of finance for best effect?

- Are you clear about your objectives from either bank finance or other sources of finance?

- Are you clear about theirs?

- How regular is your contact with your bank (or other investors)?

- When did you last question whether were using the expertise and experience of the bank (or other investors) to best effect?

- How do you assess the benefits from any financing in the practice against the costs? Are you earning less from invested capital, than the financing is costing you?

6.6 How are capital investment decisions evaluated?

- When making capital investments are the objectives of the investment clearly specified?

- What sources of advice are utilised?

- How are costs and benefits of the investment calculated?

- How are sources of funding for the investment identified and costed?

- Is the impact of taxation, grants and allowances accurately calculated?

- What potential cost or revenue variations are identified and what contingencies are incorporated into risk analyses?

- How is the impact of the investment on the business plans identified?

6.7 How often do you review the practice's tax position?

- How well do you understand the options available for minimising the tax liabilities of the practice?

- Are legitimate ways of minimising tax identified and used?

- How do you know you have a good working relationship with your accountant?

6.8 How regularly do you consider retirement financial planning?

- Do the existing partners expect to realise their equity capital upon retiring from the practice?

- If so, how do they plan to do it:
    - Sale of the practice as a going concern?

- Sale of equity to new partners?

- Ongoing income from funds loaned to the practice?

- Is it intended that new partners will be chosen from existing employees? If so, on what time-scale is the succession planned?

6.9 What are the critical financial aspects of succession to partnership?

It is often very flattering to be asked to become a partner; before deciding, have potential partners had an opportunity to appraise the financial state of the partnership and the risks of, as well as possible returns on, the investment they are being asked to make? The practice might like to consider key questions prospective partners should be asking themselves:

- Can they trust and work with the existing partners?

- What is the practice's profit sharing policy?

- What risks might the practice be exposed to (especially any pending or possible PI claims)?

- How confident is the new partner in the practice's strategy?

- How confident is the new partner that they will see a return on the investment they are being asked to make, and the risks they are being asked to share?

Practical Application Case Study: Practice Finance

- *How do you enhance the financial and business skills of mid-senior level professionals?*

- *How do you create real team working?*

- *How do you do this in a fun and enjoyable manner?*

This was the challenge posed by the senior management team of one of the larger international practices.

The approach adopted involved the design and management of a large-scale business simulation event for over 100 staff. Using an IT-based business model of a typical medium-sized surveying practice, teams of five, competed for business in a hypothetical market.

Costing projects, determining the margin for a particular piece of work, establishing how best to structure the firm for maximum profitability became real issues to manage. Cash flow, debt control and the appraisal of alternative investment decisions were all challenges the teams faced – not as theoretical exercises but as decision options within the simulation.

To add further realism to the event, each team member played the role of a Member of the Board of the firm. Over the period of the exercise, the team members had to deal with, individually and collectively, a range of business challenges. How do you create a well motivated group of staff? What are the costs involved? What do you do to manage your clients? What form should your strategy for the business take? What is the cost of taking different options? These and other issues were constantly faced by the groups throughout the exercise.

The final dimension to the activity was the real sense of team working that developed through the process. Each team member was intentionally selected to be the least well suited to the role – that way further learning could be gained. Also it required team members to coach and support each other in these unfamiliar situations. Unexpected visits from the real senior management of the firm added a further degree of challenge. Could you explain your business strategy to the chairman – quickly and simply – without becoming the 'weakest link'?

Practice Management

Integrated Case Study

'The First 100 Days'

'The first 100 days'

The following is a fictitious case which we've written to enable you to consider most of the issues highlighted in 'the *Guidelines*'. So imagine yourself as a new managing partner during a period following a major change in a firm – in this case a merger. How would you approach the challenge?

'*I have every faith in your abilities Jane, I know you can sort this firm out*'. Those infamous words of encouragement from John Parsons (57), the firm's senior partner, were uttered in 2002. They had echoed continually around Jane Allen's (39) head ever since.

Prior to her appointment as the new managing partner of Graysons & Hanrahan from 1 January the following year, she also had confidence in her ability to '*sort out*' this newly merged firm. Now, she felt much less clear.

Her appointment as managing partner of this medium-sized practice had come as a slight, but not totally unexpected, surprise. She had been with Graysons for 15 years. A respected professional with a reputation for being '*firm, but fair*', she had led the firm's largest department for the past four years. Under her guidance, the department had grown significantly and, prior to the merger, had accounted for over 60% of the firm's fee income.

The merger had been part necessity and part ambition. With such significant activity in a single main sector, Graysons felt more than a little exposed to a possible downturn in that sector. To compound their concerns, their reliance on three major financial institutions accounted for over 70% of their fee income in the sector. The other departments saw themselves as 'general practitioners' – and claimed to provide a single point of contact for their clients. Her fellow partners had also been with the firm for between 15 and 20 years and generally, with one or two exceptions, she had good relations with all of them. It was a comfortable place to work – not the most dynamic – but one which had enabled them to continue the long history of Graysons, which traced its roots back to the 1780s. Prior to the merger, Graysons had ten equity partners and 130 fee earners and support staff.

John Parsons, the senior partner, had held this post in his previous firm (Graysons). When they merged with Hanrahans in 2002, he had negotiated that he would continue in this role. He was well respected in the business community and internally had a reputation for '*running a tight ship*'. He did, however, hate '*administration and bureaucracy*' with a vengeance, and generally liked to be involved in '*all significant decisions*'. In the merger with Hanrahans, a deal had been reached that he would continue (until his retirement in three years time) as one of two joint senior partners of the merged firm.

Hanrahans appeared to be a good merger partner. Its professional disciplines complemented Graysons although it had grown from a very different start point. The firm was formed in 1986 by two ex-City practitioners who wanted the challenge of building a new firm from scratch. They had a reputation for being commercially aggressive and over its first 15 years the firm had doubled in size every three years. Along the way, a number of other entrepreneurial partners had joined and, prior to the merger, it had eight equity partners and some 80 fee earners and support staff. Hanrahans, however, recognised that the route to future growth lay in balancing out its more transactional work with a steady stream of non-transactional work. Graysons offered such an opportunity – albeit with some risks attached.

John Hanrahan (49), one of the two founders, now held the post of joint senior partner in the merged firm.

Jane's appointment as managing partner had been welcomed by all the partners. It was recognised by all that the firm's management structure and strategy needed '*sorting out*' and they all felt Jane would be able to deliver a solution.

As mentioned earlier, Jane was less sure of the '*solution*'. She had read recently of the critical importance of her 'first 100 days' in post. She knew that her style of operating, the decisions she made, and the processes she used to '*sort out*' the firm were under continuous observation by the other 17 partners. She felt the honeymoon period had come to an end. The initial enthusiasm and high expectations associated with her appointment were evaporating rapidly. *When was 'she' going to outline her strategy? Is 'she' up to this challenge?* These comments being largely attributable to partners who were originally from the Hanrahan side of the merger.

How would you advise a Jane Allen to operate during her first 100 days in post?

What should her key priorities be during those first 100 days?

Some issues to consider

The following summary is intended to act as a catalyst for comment on this case. It is not '*the answer*', it is simply one perspective. What would you/have you done differently?

So how should Jane manage her first 100 days? The initial pre-Christmas euphoria following her appointment has gone and the reality of the challenges ahead are now uppermost in her mind.

Appointment to managing partner (or other senior management position) can either be viewed as an exciting and potentially exhilarating opportunity, or alternatively, as an exhausting and ultimately impossible job. How you manage your initial period in office – and particularly your first 100 days will heavily influence which of these two potentially self-fulfilling prophesies wins out. Unfortunately, no easy-to-follow checklist exists, no one speaks to you about it and the 'unwritten rules' in some firms may imply that if you have to discuss it '*you clearly are not up to the job to which you have been appointed*'. Yet the processes you use and the approach you adopt in this critical phase can heavily influence your future success. So often, new appointees have to rely exclusively on their own instincts, which in some cases may suffice, but in others can lead to confusion, inefficiency and demoralisation.

So back to Jane – *what issues should she be considering?* Some of the issues you may have identified could be:

Setting expectations – establishing the mutual expectations and boundaries of the role each member of the senior team will play can be a crucial issue in this initial period. Jane may have two issues on this agenda. With two joint senior partners, – what roles will they play in the management of the firm – and what do they really expect from the managing partner? Jane may also be concerned to ensure that John ('tight ship') Parsons is clearly aware of how, and ultimately where, decisions will be reached. With John ('the entrepreneur') Hanrahan her concerns may be more focused on how growth will be managed in the future – again, how and where decisions will be reached.

Strategy – one might argue that the heart of the firm's need for someone to 'sort out this newly merged firm' is associated with a lack of a clear strategy. A key aspect of Jane's job will be to gain agreement for a review of the firm's future strategy. Following this, she might wish to undertake an intensive period of consultation and listening to staff at all levels within the firm. Her ability to suspend judgement during this phase whilst providing a sense of direction and emphasising the need for change in a number of areas is likely to be critical. She will need to deal with the dilemma of 'communicating your vision' – which many wish to see now, with a need to involve others at all levels in the process of establishing a joint shared sense of direction.

Service(s) – a central part of the review process will be likely to revolve around the service range which the firm is, and should be, offering in the future. The reliance of the firm on three financial institutions for 42% of its fee income would require further investigation. How well are these clients currently managed? What is happening in their business and how might the firm be affected by any changes? Should the firm expand in this sector or diversify? If the latter, in what direction?

Systems – one issue which Jane might explore in her first 100 days could be the compatibility of the systems used by the merger partners. The firm appears to be lacking in cohesiveness – the two cultures are very different and some practical steps are required to help create a common culture from the co-existing cultures. Focusing on an audit of policies and systems with a view towards creating an integration plan could be a means of starting this process.

Structure – firms which appoint new managing partners, particularly in the circumstances described in this case, do so with the anticipation of change. The most obvious, but potentially most contentious, area is that of structure. Moving too quickly to change the structure without a clear rationale may lead to a new structure on paper but the status quo pattern is likely to re-establish itself. Wait too long and the opportunity will have gone. Unless in crisis conditions, the first 100 days is more likely to be a period of listening and testing the structure against the future strategy and service plan. But, soon after the honeymoon some decisions will be expected and required. Whether the tool you use during implementation is a 'big bang sledge hammer' or 'incremental scalpel' is ultimately where your judgement will be tested.

Symbolism – during your first 100 days (and beyond!) your actions will be under the spotlight – who is seen, where, how often and when, will be noticed. Small gestures will take on much more significance in this phase than at later stages. Try and avoid, unless you are in deep financial trouble, the classic, symbolic, cost cutting moves such as 'cancel biscuits for all internal meetings' or 'stop all non-reclaimable travel', etc. This process can, however, be used in a positive sense. Changing the process by which you communicate or consult, from paper to face-to-face, will send signals about how you are likely to operate after your initial period. Be seen around the office despite your desire to get behind the figures and spend time in your office.

Segment(ing) – during any change process such as this, Jane will need to make some judgements on the level of support (or otherwise) she can expect from those who will be affected by the changes she may be introducing. Segmenting the population into:

- those she can change now
- those she can influence now
- those she can't change or influence *yet*, and
- those who can't or won't change,

may help her to gauge at various stages where her problem people exist.

Finally, Jane *may* have a more challenging issue on her mind, the need for *support* – a mentor, a 'critical friend', someone outside the firm who can act as a sounding board and help work through the managerial and political dilemmas which will inevitably arise.

Practice
Management
Guideline 7

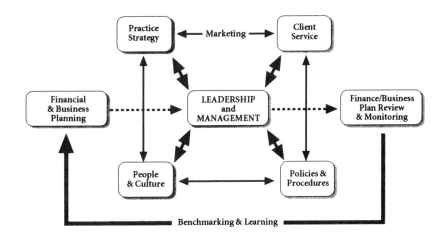

Starting Up

*What are
the essential points?*

What if you are starting up?

During the initial workshops, several people commented that we should try to produce a 'mini guideline' for those considering establishing a start-up practice to trade on their own. In today's economic world the temptations to start on your own are becoming greater. For example, you may have developed a particular expertise and/or client base. You might want a career change and greater autonomy. In some cases, going it alone may seem the only option. The advice of several agencies (commercial and government sponsored), to say nothing of banks and other financial service providers, tends to stress the potential upside of being your own boss. What about it?

7.1 Are you, and any family/partners who have a stake in your future, prepared for the change to self-employment?

- Why do you, and your partners if you have them, want to establish an independent practice?

- What steps have you taken to understand the work demanded and the risks involved?

- How competent do you feel about marketing, administering and financially managing your own practice?

- Have you spoken to, or worked with, others who have succeeded in setting up in business on their own account?

- Have you committed these ideas to paper in the form of a business plan which includes:

    - the objectives of those involved

    - the objectives of the practice

    - the marketing investment

    - how your service will be delivered

    - your plans for accommodation and administrative support

    - your personnel plan, and

    - a budget and cash flow forecast?

7.2 Have you identified a strategic niche?

What gives your initial trading advantage:

- Knowledge of a particular niche in the professional services market?

- Knowledge of the needs of a particular set of clients?

- A network of potential, or actual, clients to get you started?

- How do you assess if the demand for these services is what you think it will be?

- What will you do if it is not?

- Who are your competitors?

- Why is your service going to be different?

7.3 How are you going to market your practice?

- What marketing outlets do you have (for example, networks of key contacts, a reputation, or an established presence as a seminar speaker)?

- What else do you plan to do to market yourself?

- Is this activity budgeted for?

- How will you know if it is working?

7.4 How are you going to ensure the participation of whoever you need to work with?

Do your plans assume:

- One or more partners in the practice from day one?

- The assistance and support of family members?

- The support and custom of your initial clients?

- The services of one or more associates?

- If so, why should those people have an interest in supporting your plans? Are you clear what that interest is?

- What might go wrong?

7.5 What policies and procedures do you need from day one?

- How will you assess whether you are providing clients with the services they expect and want?

- Have you established the administrative systems you will need?

- Have you established the Quality Assurance system you will need?

- Have you a formal agreement with any partners who will work with you?

- Have you a relationship with an accountant from whom you feel you will receive a reasonable service?

- Have you budgeted for, and acquired, the office equipment that you will need to start trading?

- Have you established a simple format for contracting the services of any associates who will work with you?

- Have you established what advice and guidance is available locally through the RICS, the Chamber of Commerce or local services such as Business Link offices?

- Have you researched the support and advice available from banks, and others, whose own business interest is for you to start a business?

- What systems will you have to put in place in the first year or two of trading to ensure that your plans for years three and onwards are feasible? (Many start-up practices reach a saturation point where the founders can no longer do everything, but the risk of investing in support staff or juniors seems too large to take. Then they hit the buffers.)

7.6 Have you sorted out a budget for year 1 and a plan for years 2 and 3?

- When will your cash flow become positive?

- How sensitive is your forecast to your assumptions about the market, and the speed with which clients will pay you?

- What investment of time or capital are you making? How will you check that you are getting the return that you want?

- What level of income do you need to reach:

    - A break-even point for your practice?

    - A return commensurate with the time you will be putting in?

    - A return on any loans or other finance that you will be raising and investing in the practice?

- How will you be measuring the performance of the practice and your progress against your plans?

- Where do you want the practice to be in three years time? What needs to happen in the next 12 months to ensure that you make it?

Practice
Management
Appendices

Appendix 1

IIP: the Investors In People standards

Investors In People (IIP) is a national initiative that, like ISO 9000, has attracted critics as well as fans. For some practices that have gained the award, it has enabled them to achieve improved business performance, for others it has proved to have been a waste of time and effort, or a paper trail.

The standard is awarded through the local Training and Enterprise Council (or LEC in Scotland) on the basis that a practice is assessed as measuring up to the following standards.

- A public commitment to develop all its employees to meet its business objectives.
- Public commitment from the most senior levels.
- Employees at all levels are aware of the broad aims and vision of the organisation.
- A written but flexible plan exists setting out business goals and targets.
- Identification in the plan of broad development needs and specifications of how those will be met.
- What employees at all levels will contribute to the success of the organisation has been communicated effectively to them.
- Ensure the training and development needs of all employees are regularly reviewed.
- A written plan which identifies the resources that will be used to meet training and development needs.
- Systems to ensure training and development needs are regularly reviewed against business objectives.
- Managers who are competent to carry out their responsibilities for developing people.
- Targets and standards for development actions.
- Where appropriate, training standards are linked to achieving external standards, particularly NVQs/ SVQs.
- Actions to train and develop individuals, on recruitment and throughout their employment.
- Evaluated their investment in training and development to assess achievement and improve future effectiveness.
- Evaluated how development of people is contributing to business goals and targets.
- Evaluated whether its development actions have achieved their objectives.
- Evaluated outcomes of training and development at individual, team and organisational levels.
- Communicated the continuing commitment of top management to developing people.

Appendix 2

Making it happen

Setting aside time to plan your practice development will inevitably be difficult to achieve during the Monday to Friday period. It might, however be possible to plan, given advance warning, an initial one day 'retreat', preferably to take place 'off site'. Indeed, you may already have such events within your existing calendar. To help you think about such an activity a generic outline for such a day is outlined below. It should, however, be emphasised that each event will be different and require tailoring to emphasise issues of particular importance to the participants.

Designing a workshop to develop your practice

Assuming that it is possible to allocate an initial day to the activity, the following approach might be helpful. Each phase of the programme will involve a review of particular aspects of the data collected through the use of the questions in the *Guidelines*. In advance of the event, it would also be helpful if you or an external facilitator were able to summarise the main trends which have become apparent from a consolidation of the responses from those attending the workshop.

Introduction, objectives and review of expectations [30 minutes]

It is important that a preliminary set of objectives is established for the event. Before proceeding further it is important to gain agreement to these from those attending. The objectives might include some, or all, of the following topics:

- to review your current position in the market place

- to identify your strengths and weaknesses, together with the opportunities and threats facing you at present and in the future

- to develop a shared sense of purpose which will help shape your future direction, and

- to begin to clarify what your competitive edge is/will be in your key services and for the practice as a whole.

Where are you now? – A review of your current market position
[2 hours]

This part of the workshop will involve an examination of the perceptions of the participants towards their:

Reputation – with whom and why does the practice enjoy a particular reputation for a particular type of service?

Competitive position – how well are you doing in your chosen marketplace(s)?

Market trends – is the practice aware of and preparing for the changes which will impact on the business.

Overall strengths, weaknesses, opportunities and threats – this section of the workshop will benefit from your responses to the questions in *Guidelines 1* (Practice Strategy), *2* (Client Service and Marketing) and *4* (Learning through Benchmarking).

Where do you intend to get to? A consideration of some options for the future [2 hours]

This third phase of the workshop will enable those attending to discuss and identify a focus for the future of the practice by considering:

Focus and vision – is it possible to reach some consensus on a common purpose for the practice?

Marketing and business development – is the message the practice is conveying to its clients distinctive and clearly understood?

This section of the workshop could also benefit from a review of your responses to some of the questions in *Guidelines 1* (Practice Strategy), *2* (Client Service and Marketing) and *4* (Learning through Benchmarking).

What might be stopping you? [2 hours]

Before moving into the final stage of this initial workshop it is important to recognise and take note of any areas of resistance which might exist and to uncover any 'unwritten rules' and assumptions which might limit your chances of success. To assist it can be useful to review the responses to:

Self awareness – which taken for granted perceptions of the world might need to be challenged if a new strategy is to be adopted?

People and capabilities – have we taken stock of the capabilities of our team(s) and how these match with our strategy?

The responses to the questions in *Guidelines 3* (People and Culture) and *4* (Training and Development) will be of particular benefit.

Policies and procedures – do we need to review our policies and procedures in order to match these to our overall objectives. (See responses to questions in *Guideline 5.*)

Finance – how do our current financial obligations and future investment plans relate to our overall strategy? (See responses to questions in *Guideline 6.*)

Action planning [up to 1 hour]

The final stage of the process, which may have been integrated with the rest of the day, is action planning. This might involve inviting volunteers (or pressed people!) to co-ordinate further work. Alternatively, if this has been discussed throughout the day, it will be simply a process of confirming who will do what and by when.

Developing your practice is an iterative process. The result of this exercise will be a much clearer and more explicit, shared understanding of a more limited number of options open to the practice. From this will develop new ways of viewing the future and possibly new opportunities to be explored. It is important that this momentum is maintained and a follow up session, involving all of those attending this initial event, should take place within four to six weeks. Ideally, the follow up event should also take place off site, so maintaining, hopefully, a different atmosphere for the exercise from that normally associated with more formal business meetings.

The success of the exercise might benefit from the use of a skilled facilitator. Poorly managed workshops of this type can lead to a confused and frustrating experience. Good facilitation on the other hand can ensure the event is an enlightening and uplifting experience, providing new insights, possibilities and action.

Good luck!

Appendix 3

Authors

Dr Tom Kennie, MBA, MAppSci, MIPD, FRICS
Ranmore Consulting Group
Dunley Hill Court
Ranmore Nr. Dorking
Surrey RH5 6SX

Tel: 01483 283040
Fax: 01483 281228
e-mail: tkennie@ranmore.co.uk
www.ranmore.co.uk

Professor If Price
Facilities Management Graduate Centre
Sheffield Hallam University
Unit 7 Science Park
Sheffield S1 1WB

Tel: 0114 225 4032
Fax: 0114 225 4038
e-mail: i.price@shu.ac.uk
www.shu.ac.uk/fmgc

Contributing practices and partners

Darroll Harrison Partnership (DHP)
Paul Walker

Drake & Kannemeyer
Edward Kannemeyer

Dunster & Morton
Mike Faulkes (now retired)

J B Marks & Partners (now C M Parker Brown)
Leslie Eckett

Nigel Rose & Partners
Richard Colston

C M Parker Browne
Dennis Ulyet

Rogers Chapman plc
Trevor Saunders

Roy Ilott & Associates
Roy Ilott

Sterling Surveys Ltd
Michael Mullin

Tuffin Ferraby & Taylor
David Tuffin

Vail Williams
Ken Williams

Others who contributed to the original project
Mike Green, Sheffield Hallam University
Keith Winter, Consultant
Carolyn Slater, RICS
Joanna Thomson-Edge, (previously CPD Co-ordinator, RICS).

Particular thanks are due to *Chris Ward* of Ranmore Consulting Group for his expertise on financial management and authorship of *Guideline 6: Background Principles*.

Bibliography

These books can be obtained on loan from the RICS Library at 12 Great George Street, London SW1P 3AD. The RICS Library can be contacted by telephone on 020 7334 3749 or by fax on 020 7334 3784 or by e-mail on library@rics.org.uk.

Greenhalgh, B. (Ed) (1997) *Practice Management for Land, Construction & Property Professionals* E & FN Spoon, London

Lowendahl, B.R. (1997) *Strategic Management of Professional Service Firms* Copenhagen Business School Press

Lorsch, J.W. and Tierney, T.J. (2002) *Aligning the Stars – How to Succeed When Professionals Drive Results* Harvard Business School Press

Maister, D.H. (2001) *Practice What You Preach* The Free Press, New York

Maister, D.H. (1997) *True Professionalism* The Free Press, New York

Maister, D.H. (1993) *Managing the Professional Service Firm* The Free Press, New York

Maister, D.H., Green, C.H. and Galford, R.M. (2000) *The Trusted Advisor* The Free Press, New York

Mayson, S. (1997) *Making Sense of Law Firms* Blackstone Press, London

McKenna, P.J. and Maister, D.H. (2002) *First Among Equals – How to Manage a Group of Professionals* The Free Press, New York

Parry, R. (1991) *People Businesses. Making Professional Firms Profitable* Business Books Ltd, London

Other useful texts

Bennis, W. (1998) *Managing People is Like Herding Cats* Kogan Page, London

Forsyth, P. (1999) *Marketing Professional Services* Kogan Page, London

Goleman, D. (1996) *Emotional Intelligence* Bloomsbury, London

Gratton, L. (2000) *Living Strategy – Putting People at the Heart of Corporate Purpose* Financial Times/Prentice Hall, London

Kaplan, R.S. and Norton, D.P. (1996) *The Balanced Scorecard* Harvard Business School Press

Kay, J. (1994) *The Foundations of Corporate Success* Oxford University Press

Manzoni, J-P. and Barsoux, J-L. (2002) *The Set-Up-To-Fail Syndrome* Harvard Business School Press

Price, I. and Shaw, R. (1998) *Shifting the Patterns* Management Books 2000, London

Price, I. (1996) *A Plain Persons Guide to Benchmarking* Guide produced by the Facilities Management Graduate Centre, Sheffield Hallam University

Quinn, J.B. (1992) *Intelligent Enterprise* Free Press, New York

Ringland, G. (1998) *Scenario Planning – Management for the Future* Wiley, Chichester

Schwartz, P. (1991) *The Art of the Long View* Wiley, Chichester

Scott (1998) *The Intellect Industry* Wiley, Chichester

Scott-Morgan, P. (1996) *The Unwritten Rules of the Game* Blackwell, Oxford

Schneider, B. and Bowen, D.E. (1995) *Winning the Service Game* Harvard Business School Press

Senge, P. (1990) *The Fifth Discipline:* The Art and Practice of the Learning Organisation, New York

van der Heijden, K. (1997) *Scenarios: The Art of Strategic Conversation* Wiley, Chichester

Walker, K., Ferguson, C. and Denvir, P. (1998) *Creating New Clients. Marketing & Selling Professional Services* Cassell

Video resources

In addition to the written resource materials mentioned above and throughout the text, some short videos have been produced on a number of aspects of the material in the study guide. These include:

Kennie, T. and Price, I. (1996) *Developing a Strategic Plan for Your Firm* Television Education Network, Successful Management for Professional Firms Series – Module 1

Kennie, T. and Andrews, B. (1996) *Providing Outstanding Client Service* Television Education Network, Successful Management for Professional Firms Series – Module 1

Kennie, T., Price, I. and Middlehurst, R. (1996) *Leading Professionals – Conducting the Feline Orchestra* Television Education Network, Successful Management for Professional Firms Series – Module 3

Kennie, T. (1999) *Practice Management – Structuring for Growth* Legal Network Television, Programme 591, The College of Law

Online Resources

http://www.occupier.org is a site created by Sheffield Hallam University's Facilities Management Centre, under contract to the RICS Foundation to act as a review of current public domain knowledge concerning the impact of property related initiatives on occupiers business performance. It contains a wealth of links to other online material.

Learning Resources
Centre